The
WOULD-BE
INVALID

NEW CENTURY CLASSICS

NEW CENTURY CLASSICS

The
WOULD-BE
INVALID

Le Malade Imaginaire

MOLIERE

*Translated and edited
by MORRIS BISHOP*

APPLETON-CENTURY, NEW YORK

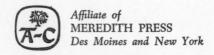

Affiliate of
MEREDITH PRESS
Des Moines and New York

INTRODUCTION

The printed dialogue of a play is not a play, any more than the printed score of music is music. Music does not exist until it is played, nor does a stage play exist until it is acted on a stage. Nevertheless, a musically-minded person can create music in his spirit by reading a score, and similarly an imaginative reader can create a play in his mind by reading a text properly. All reading is a creative act on the part of the reader; but the reading of a play requires more creative coöperation from the reader than do most forms of literature, except perhaps poetry.

There are two ways in which the reader can supply this creative coöperation. The first way is to imagine the characters of a play as real people, actually loving, fighting, and dying against a real background, houses, streets, battlefields, forests. This is the best way to read *Hamlet*, or *As You Like It*, or *Faust*.

The other way is to erect a theatre-stage in one's mind, and to see the characters in the drama as actors, entering and exiting, taking prescribed positions on the stage, going through their stage business, artfully mouthing their lines, and ceasing to exist when they walk off. This is the best way to read Molière.

To read in this manner requires some effort, some practice. When you read a speech, you should mentally look at the actor who is reciting it. You should have an idea what he looks like, what costume he is wearing. You should not only hear his words, you should watch his play of expression. You should see his body, the gestures of his hands. If you read a play as a series of long speeches uttered by cloudy figures standing still, you are reading it wrong. The action, the stage business, is as important as the words.

In the case of Molière, the stage business is of particular importance. Much of it was devised by Molière himself, and it has been repeated and amplified during three hundred years of an unbroken tradition. It is a part of his plays, and should be printed with the spoken words. In this edition it is. (The translator has been immeasurably aided by the edition of Pierre Valde, Paris, 1946, which reproduces his own production of the play.)

Molière's plays are above all acting plays, for he was a professional actor, whose life was totally given to the theatre.

Molière was born in Paris, in 1622, of a prosperous bourgeois family. (His real name was Jean-Baptiste Poquelin.) He was educated in the best Paris school, then he unwillingly studied law. As soon as he could escape from parental control he went on the stage. He took over a Paris theatre and organized his own company, and soon lost all his money. Defeated, he took his troupe to the provinces, and for twelve years wandered up and down France, playing in barns and indoor tennis courts, often at odds with the local authorities and police, certainly often at desperate shifts for money. He learned the actor's trade thoroughly well; he also learned a great deal about human behavior and misbehavior.

He returned to Paris in 1658. His company soon became immensely popular and gained the special approbation of King Louis XIV, who was then a gay young man in his early twenties. For fifteen years he led a life of the utmost activity, acting, directing, managing, and writing in haste 33 plays, everything from tragi-comedy to knockabout farce. His plays were written to attract and hold audiences, to make money; but many of them have become the glories of the French theatre.

Le Malade imaginaire, The Would-Be Invalid, was his last play. At the fourth performance, on 17 February, 1673, Molière, who played Argan, was seized with a hemorrhage

of the lungs during the final scene (the first *Juro*, p. 80).
He succeeded in playing out the scene, and was carried
home, where he died within a few hours.

Le Malade imaginaire is a farce, or farce-comedy, with
music. It may be called as well a musical comedy, for the
songs and dances are incorporated into the story and are
justified by it. Its purpose was to amuse by the presentation
of a universally recognizable type, the hypochondriac, in a
series of comic situations which are provoked by his character.

There is no need to analyze Molière's comic devices. Most
of them were traditional in Molière's time; all of them are
in common use today. But the modern reader must be struck
by the fact that Molière knew all the current tricks of the
comedian: the cumulative effect of repetition, the change of
pace, the big word, the double-take, dignity's pratfall, and
so on. Molière, in fact, set the model for the farce, as we may
see it today in any two-reeler from Hollywood.

In *Le Malade imaginaire* Molière uses his farcical tech-
nique for a special purpose: to burlesque the practice of medicine in his time. For this reason the play has been called, a
little pompously, a thesis play. Even more pompously, it
has been termed a social comedy in that it depicts the dis-
integrating effects of a monomania on a bourgeois household.
These claims may be well sustained, but they need not be
argued here. For *Le Malade imaginaire* is nearly always
played as broad farce, and broad farce it remains in every
Frenchman's mind.

What must, however, strike any modern reader is the bitterness of Molière's mockery of the practice of medicine; and
the reader may well regard Molière's hatred and distrust of
medicine as unreasonable.

But in point of fact, the state of medicine in 1670 was
enough to horrify us, as well as Molière. The education of a
physician was entirely theoretical, almost entirely based on

ancient authority. He had no clinical training; the young Doctor might gain his degree without ever having seen a sick man. An occasional dissection was held, when an executed criminal could be had from the police; but the lecturer contented himself with pointing out the various organs with a wand, while a barber-surgeon did the grisly work. The medical student was esteemed chiefly for his skill in abstract argument, for his readiness in citing classic authorities, and for the fluency of his Latin. He presented three theses for his degree; these were printed, often with an allegorical picture. (See p. 33.) They dealt with such subjects as these: Is sneezing a natural act? Is it salutary to get drunk once a month? Should one have one's hair cut with regard to the phases of the moon? Is woman an imperfect work of nature?

The pedants of the Faculty set their faces firmly against any innovation, for innovation was denial of the authority of Galen and Hippocrates. While in England Harvey had discovered the circulation of the blood, the Paris Faculty of Medicine treated his appeal to observation with contempt. You will note that young Thomas Diafoirus has written a thesis against the presumptuous holders of such theories. (See p. 33.)

The average physician relied on three sovereign therapeutic methods: bleeding, purging, and enemas, to cleanse the body of its noisome humors.

Blood flowed in torrents. Guy Patin, a great authority of his day, bled an infant three days old; a child of seven, thirteen times in two weeks; his own son, twenty times for a persistent fever; one patient, sixty-four times for rheumatism; and a man of eighty, eleven times in six days. In one year, the physician of Louis XIII prescribed for him 47 bleedings, 212 purges, and 215 enemas. The King died young. Such examples are merely characteristic. We may recognize that Molière's distrust of the doctors was reasonable indeed.

Purges and enemas of incredible violence were prescribed.

The literature of the period is full of horrible examples, too horrible to be given here. Enemas, or clysters, were commonly administered by apothecaries. Hence the apothecaries lent themselves to gross comedy, and their badge of office, the syringe, was the most ludicrous of instruments.

In view of the facts, then, Molière's reliance on nature as against contemporary medicine seems far from foolish. But we must recognize that new facts have replaced old facts. The experimental attitude, which was barely taking shape in Molière's time, was soon to alter the whole aspect of medical science.

Molière had the most serious personal grievance against the doctors. His wandering actor's life, with its nervous tension, its irregular, hasty meals, had given him a chronic nervous indigestion. Later, he contracted tuberculosis. He was obliged to carry on his multifarious and exhausting activity while his health gradually failed, while the physicians proposed only treatment that would weaken him further. He saw old friends die of reckless bleeding and purging. In 1672, just before he wrote *Le Malade imaginaire*, his only son, a year-old baby, suddenly died. We may suppose that this sick, despairing man blamed the doctors, when he called upon them in vain to save his son's life.

Under the broad farce of *Le Malade imaginaire* there is, then, a hidden tragedy of sickness and death, the tragedy of Molière. This tragedy must be present to the mind of a modern reader who has learned to know and love Molière's spacious spirit. He drew a wry, agonizing pleasure from putting in his plays confessions which would be imperceptible to any casual auditors, phrases and implications which were meant for himself alone. He is not the only man who has found a torturing satisfaction in presenting his secret self to the public, in such a disguise that only the initiated may recognize it.

Today we who know Molière can penetrate the disguise. Béralde's confidence in nature (Act III) is Molière's own.

When Argan, who was played by Molière in person, prophesies that the physicians will let Molière die untended in return for his railleries, he was foreseeing his own unhappy case. When Béralde says that Molière has only strength enough to bear his illness, he makes a statement of tragic truth. When, in the scene with Toinette, in Act III, Argan describes his symptoms, Molière is diagnosing his own actual troubles. "The lungs, the lungs!" cries Toinette; and she is quite right. When, during the course of the play, he was seized by his consumptive cough, he was able to pass it off as a bit of intentional comedy.

It is all very painful. And it makes the tragedy of *Le Malade* who is not *imaginaire*: the tragedy of the actor who dresses his dying hours in motley, who turns his face to mankind, with laughter on his lips for human folly, as the final curtain is drawn.

THE PRINCIPAL DATES
IN MOLIÈRE'S LIFE

1622 Birth of Jean-Baptiste Poquelin (Molière), in Paris on January 15.

1639 Finishes studies at Collège de Clermont, Paris.

1641 Receives law degree, enters father's upholstering business.

1643 Establishes Illustre Théâtre, Paris.

1645 Molière's troupe, bankrupt, leaves Paris for provinces.

1653 *L'Étourdi*, first original play, staged in Lyon.

1658 Molière's troupe returns to Paris.

1659 *Les Précieuses ridicules*, first successful play.

1662 Marriage to Armande Béjart, actress.

1662 *L'École des femmes.*

1663 Molière receives pension from Louis XIV, as indication of court favor.

1664 *Tartuffe.*

1665 *Don Juan, ou le Festin de pierre.*

1666 *Le Misanthrope.*

1666 *Le Médecin malgré lui.*

1668 *L'Avare.*

1670 *Le Bourgeois gentilhomme.*

1672 *Les Femmes savantes.*

1673 *Le Malade imaginaire.*

1673 Death of Molière, on February 17, at close of fourth performance of *Le Malade imaginaire*.

THE CAST

[The specifications of costume are taken mostly from seventeenth-century editions of the play.]

ARGAN, a prosperous bourgeois. He wears a nightcap with lace crown, a neckerchief carelessly knotted, a red dressing-jacket with lace or braid, tight knee-breeches, heavy stockings, slippers.

BÉLINE, Argan's second wife, considerably younger than he. Good-looking elegant dress of the period.

ANGÉLIQUE, Argan's daughter by his first marriage. Attractive young-girl costume of the period.

LOUISON, Argan's daughter by his first marriage. She is about 6.

BÉRALDE, Argan's brother. Sober gentleman's costume.

CLÉANTE, in love with Angélique. Costumed as fine young gentleman of the period. He wears a curled, flowing wig.

MONSIEUR DIAFOIRUS, physician. He wears formal dress of seventeenth-century physician: a long, flowing black robe, a large wig, and a toque, or brimless cylindrical hat about 8 inches high, encircled with varicolored rings of bright velvet.

THOMAS DIAFOIRUS, his son. Same costume as his father, but with plain broad white collar. Instead of a wig, he wears his own hair, plastered to his skull.

MONSIEUR PURGON, physician. Dressed like Monsieur Diafoirus.

MONSIEUR FLEURANT, apothecary. Dressed in black or gray-brown gown, and wig. No hat.

MONSIEUR DE BONNEFOI, notary. Dressed in formal black.

TOINETTE, maidservant. Dainty, sprightly, but not elaborate house dress.

The
WOULD-BE
INVALID

PROLOGUE

[At the first production, in February, 1673, the performance opened with an allegorical ballet, celebrating the recent military triumphs of Louis XIV in Holland. The text is omitted here.]

ACT I

[All the action takes place in ARGAN's bedroom. The most conspicuous feature of the setting is an enormous four-poster bed, on the spectator's right. It stands on a platform, raised one step above the stage level. On the spectator's left is ARGAN's easy chair. Near at hand is a table, loaded with medicines. Also a small portable table, and chairs. At rear of stage, three steps leading up to a small platform, with a curtain masking the rear entrance. This is the entrance for visitors from outside the house. The actors coming from other rooms in the house, or going to them, enter and exit at either side. Practicable doors are unnecessary; the exits may be masked by curtains.

As the curtain rises, ARGAN is found sitting in his easy chair, wearing a dressing-jacket. He is a ruddy, vigorous-looking man, capable of quick and excited action, with which his exaggerated airs of illness make a humorous contrast. On the small table before him are a large ledger, an inkwell, a quill pen, a glass of water, two bowls. He is

1

*reading a druggist's bill. As he completes each addition he
takes the proper number of counters from a bowl and drops
them in the second bowl. He reads the items of the druggist's
bill in a rapid, chanting monotone.*]

ARGAN Three and two is five and five is ten and ten is
twenty. Three and two is five. [*He drops a handful of counters in the second bowl, utters a sound of relief, takes a drink
of water, gargles long and loud, spits into a bowl beside him
on the floor. Reads from the druggist's bill.*] "Item, on the
twenty-fourth, a little enema, insinuating, emollient, alleviat-
ing, [*he enjoys the phrases*] to mollify, humidify, and refresh
the intestinal tract of the gentleman." What I like about the
bills from Monsieur Fleurant the apothecary is that they are
always so respectful. "The intestinal tract of the gentleman,
thirty sous." [*He realizes after a moment the high price.*]
Yes, but Monsieur Fleurant, it is not enough to be respectful, you must also be reasonable and not swindle the sick.
Thirty sous for an enema! I am your very humble servant,
but I won't pay it. In your other bills you put them down at
twenty sous, and when a druggist says twenty sous, he really
means ten sous. Here they are, ten sous. [*Drops counters in
bowl. Reads*] "Plus, on the same day, a good detergent
enema, composed of double catholicon, rhubarb, honey, et
cetera, according to prescription, to cleanse, purify, and ex-
purgate the intestinal tract of the gentleman, thirty sous."
With your kind permission, ten sous. "Plus, on the same day,
in the evening, an hepatic julep, soporific and somniferous,
compounded to induce sleep in the gentleman, thirty-five
sous." I don't complain of that, for it did put me to sleep.
Ten, fifteen, sixteen, seventeen sous, six farthings. "Plus, on
the twenty-fifth, a fine purgative tonic, compounded of fresh
cassia with levantine senna and other drugs, according to the
prescription of Doctor Purgon, to expel and evacuate the
bile of the gentleman, four francs." [*With incredulous fury*]
Yes, but Monsieur Fleurant, you are going too far, your
patients have got to live, haven't they? Doctor Purgon

didn't order you to put down four francs. Three francs, put down three francs, if you please. And a half of that is thirty sous. [*Drops counters in bowl.*] "Plus, on the same day, an anodine astringent potion, to relax the gentleman, thirty sous." Good; fifteen sous. "Plus, on the twenty-sixth, a carminative enema, to reduce the gentleman's gas, thirty sous." Let's say ten sous, Monsieur Fleurant. "Plus the gentleman's enema repeated in the evening, as above, thirty sous." My dear Monsieur Fleurant, ten sous. "Plus, on the twenty-seventh, a good medicine designed to hasten elimination, and to banish the gentleman's humors, three francs." A half of that is thirty sous. [*His anger has dwindled; he pauses, wipes his brow, resumes his reckoning with real gusto.*] I am glad you're more reasonable. "Plus, on the twenty-eighth, a compound of whey, clarified and sweetened, to dulcify, mollify, temper and refresh the gentleman's blood, twenty sous." Good, ten sous. "Plus a cordial and preservative potion, composed of twelve grains of bezoar-stone, syrup of lemon and pomegranate, and other ingredients according to prescription, five francs." Ah, Monsieur Fleurant, wait a minute, please. If you treat people that way, who's going to get sick? Content yourself with four francs. Twenty, forty sous. Three and two is five and five is ten and ten is twenty. Sixty-three francs four sous six farthings. So this month I have taken one, two, three, four, five, six, seven, eight purges, and one, two, three, four, five, six, seven, eight, nine, ten, eleven, twelve enemas. And last month, there were twelve purges and twenty enemas. No wonder I'm not so well this month as I was last month. I'll tell that to Doctor Purgon, he'll fix it. . . . Come now, take all this stuff away. [*He shuts his ledger and waits for someone to execute his order. Silence. He looks in both directions.*] Nobody here! There's no use my talking, they always go and leave me alone. There's no way to keep them around. [*He rings the small bell on his table.*] They don't hear anything, and my bell doesn't make enough noise. [*He rings bell and shouts at the same time, getting steadily more angry.*] Jingle, jingle,

jingle, jingle! No use. Jingle, jingle, jingle, jingle! They're deaf! Toinette! Jingle, jingle, jingle! I might just as well not be ringing at all. Shameless hussy! Jingle, jingle, jingle! You'll drive me crazy! [*He throws bell on the floor, in a fury.*] Jingle, jingle, jingle, the devil take you, you slut! Is it possible that they can leave a poor invalid alone like that? Jingle, jingle, jingle; it's really sad. Jingle, jingle, jingle! Good heavens, they're going to leave me here alone to die! [*Feebly, as a last appeal for help*] Jingle, jingle, jingle!

[*Enter* TOINETTE. *She is the soubrette, the pert parlor-maid, who has a secure place in the household.*]

TOINETTE All right, here I am.

ARGAN [*collapsing, fanning his face with handkerchief*] Oh, you slut! Oh, you hussy!

TOINETTE [*comes downstage, beside* ARGAN's *chair. Recognizes she is about to be scolded, and takes her defensive measures*] The deuce take your impatience! You made me rush so I gave my head a terrible bang on a shutter.

ARGAN [*feebly*] You scoundrel—

TOINETTE [*interrupting*] Oh—oh—

ARGAN It's been already—

TOINETTE Oh—oh—

ARGAN It's been an hour already—

TOINETTE Oh—oh—

ARGAN You left me alone—

TOINETTE Oh—oh—

ARGAN [*shouting above* TOINETTE's *wails*] Shut up, you hag, and let me give you a good going over.

TOINETTE Yes, that's a nice idea, after the way I hurt myself.

ARGAN [*feebly*] You made me yell myself hoarse, you rascal.

TOINETTE And you made me bump my head, so we're even. We'll call it off, if you like.

ARGAN What, you hussy?

TOINETTE Oh—oh—

ARGAN You little devil! You would—

TOINETTE Oh—oh—

ARGAN [*surrendering*] What! I won't even have the pleasure of scolding her!

TOINETTE [*turning suddenly sweet*] Scold all you like; I don't mind.

ARGAN [*furiously*] You don't let me, you devil, by interrupting me all the time.

TOINETTE [*reasonably*] If you have the pleasure of scolding me, I certainly ought to have the pleasure of crying. That's fair, isn't it? [ARGAN *prepares to protest;* TOINETTE *begins to howl.*] Oh—oh— [ARGAN *gives up, and puts his hands over his ears.*]

ARGAN All right, all right; let it go. Take all this stuff away, you rapscallion; take it away. [TOINETTE *picks up the small table and starts off.* ARGAN *seizes her by the arm.*] Did my enema today come out well?

TOINETTE Your enema?

ARGAN Yes. Was there much bile?

TOINETTE Goodness, I don't worry about those things. That's up to Monsieur Fleurant, since he gets his money out of it.

[*She sets the table down.*]

ARGAN [*offended*] Anyway, be sure and get some hot water ready for the enema I'll have to take soon.

TOINETTE [*comes back beside* ARGAN's *chair*] That Monsieur Fleurant and that Doctor Purgon, they're making a fool out of you and that nasty old body of yours. They're milking you like a cow. I'd like to ask them what's wrong with you really, to make you take so much medicine and things.

[*She picks up the bowl from the floor and puts it under the medicine table.*]

ARGAN Shut up, stupid. It isn't your business to criticize the conclusions of medical science. Send in my daughter Angélique. There's something I want to tell her.

TOINETTE [*moving to the rear, sees* ANGÉLIQUE, *offstage*] She's coming of her own accord. She guessed what you were thinking.

[*Enter* ANGÉLIQUE. *She comes downstage.*]

ARGAN Come here, Angélique. I am glad you came in; I wanted to talk to you.

ANGÉLIQUE I am glad to hear what you have to say.

[*She stands beside his chair.*]

ARGAN [*contorts himself violently*] No. Wait a minute. Give me my stick. I'll be right back.

[TOINETTE *comes from behind his chair, helps him to rise, gives him his stick, takes him under the arm, and helps him out, at a hobbling run. She returns alone.*]

TOINETTE Hurry up, sir, hurry. Monsieur Fleurant gives us plenty to do.

[*She goes to bed, begins to make it up.*]

ANGÉLIQUE [*confidentially, in fear that her father may return*] Toinette!

TOINETTE What?

ANGÉLIQUE Look at me a minute.

[*She looks shyly at audience.* TOINETTE *straightens up, stares at* ANGÉLIQUE.]

TOINETTE All right. I'm looking at you.

ANGÉLIQUE [*sighs*] Toinette!

TOINETTE What do you mean, "Toinette"?

ANGÉLIQUE Don't you guess what I want to talk about?

TOINETTE I can guess all right. About our young lover. [*She resumes her bedmaking.*] He's been our only subject of conversation for a week, and if you don't talk about him all the time, I know something's wrong.

ANGÉLIQUE [*turning to* TOINETTE] Since you know that, why don't you bring the subject up of your own accord?

TOINETTE [*stops her work*] You never give me time. I never can get ahead of you.

ANGÉLIQUE I admit that I never seem to tire of talking about him, and it makes my heart happy to confide in you.

[TOINETTE *goes back to work.* ANGÉLIQUE *joins her on the far side of the bed.* TOINETTE *tucks in the bedclothes. After each speech, she pushes* ANGÉLIQUE *along, as she tucks in the bed.* ANGÉLIQUE, *in a glassy-eyed trance, makes no objection.*] But tell me, Toinette, do you condemn the feeling that I have for him?

TOINETTE Far from it.

ANGÉLIQUE Am I wrong in abandoning myself to these sweet emotions?

TOINETTE I don't say that at all.

ANGÉLIQUE Would you expect me to be absolutely insensible to all the tender protestations of ardent passion he makes to me?

TOINETTE [*finishes tucking in the far side of the bed, passes in front of* ANGÉLIQUE, *begins tucking in the near side*] Heavens, no.

ANGÉLIQUE [*joins* TOINETTE. *Same business.*] Just tell me, don't you think there is something fateful, something almost supernatural, in the extraordinary way we met?

TOINETTE Yes.

ANGÉLIQUE Don't you think that the way he came to my defense without knowing me marks him as a really gallant gentleman?

TOINETTE Yes.

ANGÉLIQUE And that no one could have acted in a more honorable way?

TOINETTE I agree entirely.

ANGÉLIQUE That there was something very polished about his manners?

TOINETTE Oh, yes, yes.

[*She goes to head of bed, arranges pillows.*]

ANGÉLIQUE [*turns shyly away, toward audience*] Toinette, don't you think he is really unusually good-looking?

TOINETTE Most assuredly.

ANGÉLIQUE That there's something sort of distinguished about him?

TOINETTE I certainly do.

ANGÉLIQUE That there's something noble in his language, just as there is in his actions?

TOINETTE Oh, absolutely.

ANGÉLIQUE That there's a really sincere emotion in everything he says to me?

TOINETTE That's true, too.

ANGÉLIQUE [*turns impulsively to* TOINETTE] And that there's nothing more dreadful than the way they keep me shut up, so that there can be no proper expression for the mutual ardor which heaven inspires in us?

TOINETTE [*in a soothing tone*] You are absolutely right.
[*She goes to the medicine table.*]

ANGÉLIQUE [*following* TOINETTE] But dear Toinette, do you think he loves me as much as he says?

TOINETTE Hé hé! Those matters are sometimes a little open to doubt. The imitations of love look a lot like the real thing, and I have seen some people who were wonderful actors in that line.

ANGÉLIQUE [*taking* TOINETTE's *banter seriously*] Oh, Toinette, what do you mean? [TOINETTE *signals to her to talk less loud.*] Oh dear, the way he talks to me, would it be possible he weren't telling the truth?

TOINETTE [*embraces* ANGÉLIQUE] Anyway, you'll soon know the answer. Since he wrote to you yesterday that he was going to ask for your hand in marriage, you should soon find out whether he is sincere towards you or not. That will be the real proof.

ANGÉLIQUE Oh, Toinette, if he is deceiving me, I will never believe in any man as long as I live.

TOINETTE Here's your father coming back.
[*She takes her stand by the armchair and awaits him. Enter* ARGAN, *looking cheerful.* TOINETTE *inquires, in dumbshow:* "Was it all right?" ARGAN *nods.* TOINETTE *takes his stick, hangs it on the back of the chair, helps him to sit down.*]

ARGAN Well, Daughter, I am going to give you a bit of

news which will perhaps surprise you. Your hand has been requested in marriage. [ANGÉLIQUE *laughs.*] How's that? You laugh? Yes, marriage, that's a funny word. Nothing seems more laughable to girls, eh? Ah, nature, nature, human nature! As nearly as I can see, my dear, there's no use my asking you whether you want to get married.

ANGÉLIQUE Father, it is my duty to do everything it may please you to order.

[*Curtseys.*]

ARGAN I am very happy to have such an obedient daughter. So the matter is settled. I have promised your hand.

ANGÉLIQUE It is only proper, Father, that I should blindly obey all your dispositions.

[*Curtseys.*]

ARGAN [*pulls out his handkerchief*] Your stepmother wanted me to make you a nun, and so did your little sister Louison. That has been your stepmother's idea right along.

[*Blows his nose ceremoniously.*]

TOINETTE [*aside*] The old witch has her reasons.

ARGAN She didn't want to consent to this marriage; but I won out, and my word has been given.

ANGÉLIQUE Oh, Father, how grateful I am to you for all your kindness!

[*She kisses his hand.*]

TOINETTE [*moves to side of* ARGAN's *chair*] In fact, I am grateful to you too, and this is the most sensible thing you have done in your life.

[ARGAN *looks at her angrily.* TOINETTE *mimics:* "Oh, I beg your pardon!" *goes to the medicine table, and listens to the conversation.*]

ARGAN I haven't yet seen the young man in question; but they tell me that I will be very well pleased with him, and you too.

ANGÉLIQUE Oh, certainly, Father.

ARGAN What do you mean? Have you seen him?

[ANGÉLIQUE *recognizes her blunder, appeals mutely for*

help to TOINETTE. TOINETTE *signals that she should admit everything.* ARGAN *looks suspiciously at* TOINETTE, *who fusses with medicines.*]

ANGÉLIQUE [*kneels beside her father, takes his hand*] Since your consent makes it possible for me to tell you my heart's secrets, I won't conceal from you that we met quite by chance, only six days ago, and that the request for marriage you have received is the result of the liking we conceived for each other, at very first sight.

ARGAN They didn't tell me that, but I'm glad of it, and it's a good thing that's the way it was. They say he's a tall, handsome young man.

ANGÉLIQUE Yes, Father.

ARGAN Well built.

ANGÉLIQUE Oh, certainly.

ARGAN Nice manners.

ANGÉLIQUE Yes indeed.

ARGAN Good looking.

ANGÉLIQUE Very good looking.

ARGAN Well behaved; good family.

ANGÉLIQUE Absolutely.

ARGAN A decent young man.

ANGÉLIQUE Oh, as decent as can be.

ARGAN Speaks Latin and Greek well.

ANGÉLIQUE I don't know about that.

ARGAN He will become a doctor in three days.

ANGÉLIQUE Will he, Father?

ARGAN Yes. Didn't he tell you?

ANGÉLIQUE No, he didn't. Who told *you?*

ARGAN Doctor Purgon.

ANGÉLIQUE Does Doctor Purgon know him?

ARGAN What a question! Of course he knows him, since he's Doctor Purgon's nephew.

ANGÉLIQUE Cléante is Doctor Purgon's nephew?

ARGAN What Cléante? We're talking about the young man who has asked your hand in marriage.

ANGÉLIQUE Yes, exactly.

ARGAN Well, it's Doctor Purgon's nephew, who is the son of his brother-in-law, Doctor Diafoirus; and that son's name is Thomas Diafoirus, and not Cléante. [TOINETTE *claps her hand over her mouth.*] And we concluded that marriage this morning, Doctor Purgon, Monsieur Fleurant, and I. And tomorrow this new son-in-law of ours is to be brought in by his father. What's the matter? You look like a duck in a fit.

ANGÉLIQUE The fact is, Father, I know now you were talking about one person, and I thought you meant another.
                      [*She rises, and turns away from her father.*]

TOINETTE [*comes downstage, beside* ARGAN's *chair*] What, sir! You have actually done this silly thing? With all your money, you would think of marrying your daughter to a mere doctor?

ARGAN Yes. What business is it of yours, you brazen hussy?

TOINETTE Calm down; no bad language. Can't we have a reasonable argument without your getting angry? [ARGAN *moves to protest.*] There, there, let's be calm and cool. What, may I ask, is your reason for such a marriage?

ARGAN My reason is that, sick and infirm as I am, [*he forces a cough, and speaks in a whining tone*] I want to have a son-in-law and other alliances in the medical world, so that I can be assured of proper aid against illness, and so that I can have access to the necessary remedies in my own family and get full profit from consultations and prescriptions.

TOINETTE [*soothingly*] Well, that certainly is a reason, and it is really a pleasure to be able to discuss things soberly and calmly. But sir, put your hand on your conscience. Are you really sick?

ARGAN [*overcome; feebly*] What do you mean, hussy, am I really sick? [*furious; bellowing*] Am I really sick, hussy?

TOINETTE All right, all right; you're sick. Let's not dispute about that. Yes, you are very sick; I agree. Sicker than you think. [ARGAN *is startled.*] That's all settled. But your daughter is to marry a husband for herself, and as she isn't sick, it isn't necessary to give her a doctor.

ARGAN [*naïvely*] It's for me I'm giving her a doctor. [*He looks at* ANGÉLIQUE.] A proper daughter ought to be happy to marry someone who is useful to her father's health.

TOINETTE Look here, sir, would you like me to give you a bit of friendly advice?

ARGAN [*wearily*] What is this friendly advice?

TOINETTE Just give up this marriage.

ARGAN And the reason is?

TOINETTE The reason is that your daughter won't consent to it.

ARGAN She won't consent to it?

TOINETTE No.

ARGAN My daughter?

TOINETTE Your daughter. She will tell you that she has no concern with Dr. Diafoirus, nor with his son Thomas Diafoirus, nor with all the Diafoiruses in the world.

ARGAN [*shouting*] I have concern with them, I have plenty. Not to mention the fact that this is a better match than you think. Dr. Diafoirus has just that one son, who is his only heir. And besides, Dr. Purgon, who hasn't any wife or children, will leave him all his property in view of this marriage; and Dr. Purgon is a man who has a good eight thousand francs a year income.

TOINETTE He must have killed a lot of people to get so rich.

ARGAN Eight thousand francs a year is something, not to mention the father's property.

TOINETTE That's all very fine, sir; but I come back to my point just the same. I advise you, between ourselves, to choose some other husband for her; she isn't made to be Madame Diafoirus.

ARGAN [*calmly*] It is my desire that this should be the case.

TOINETTE Tut tut, don't say that.

ARGAN What do you mean, don't say that?

TOINETTE By no means.

ARGAN And why shouldn't I say it?

TOINETTE People will say that you don't know what you're talking about.

ARGAN They can say what they please, but I have given my word, and I expect her to carry it out.

TOINETTE No, I am sure she won't do it.

ARGAN I'll make her do it.

TOINETTE She won't do it, I tell you.

ARGAN She will do it, or I'll put her in a convent.

TOINETTE You?

ARGAN Me.

TOINETTE Good.

ARGAN What do you mean, good?

TOINETTE You won't put her in a convent.

ARGAN I won't put her in a convent?

TOINETTE No.

ARGAN No?

TOINETTE [shouts in ARGAN's face] No.

ARGAN [shouts in TOINETTE's face] Well, well, that's very nice! I won't put my daughter in a convent if I want to?

TOINETTE No, I tell you.

ARGAN Who will stop me?

TOINETTE You will yourself.

ARGAN [amazed] I will myself?

TOINETTE Yes. You won't have the heart to do it.

ARGAN Yes I will.

TOINETTE You're being silly.

ARGAN I am not being silly.

TOINETTE Your fatherly affection will get the better of you.

ARGAN It won't get the better of me.

TOINETTE [passes behind his chair] She'll cry a little, throw her arms around your neck [she throws her arms around ARGAN's neck from behind; he struggles] and she'll say tenderly: "Oh my dear little papa," and that will be enough to move you.

ARGAN [*shakes her off*] It won't move me a bit.

TOINETTE Yes it will!

[*She pats the top of* ARGAN's *head; he slaps at her hand.*]

ARGAN I tell you I won't change my mind.

TOINETTE [*beside* ARGAN's *chair*] Nonsense.

ARGAN Don't say nonsense.

TOINETTE Goodness, I know you. You're naturally kind.
[*She starts to walk away.*]

ARGAN [*rises, furious, walks toward* TOINETTE, *his arm uplifted to strike her*] I am not kind. I can be ugly when I want to.

TOINETTE [*protecting herself with her arm*] Careful, sir. You're forgetting you're sick.

[ARGAN *stops; he totters, turns, runs to collapse in his chair. The two women rush to his side.* TOINETTE *fetches a glass of water from medicine table;* ARGAN *drinks greedily. The two women rise up, relieved.*]

ARGAN [*feebly*] I command her absolutely to get ready to marry the husband I choose for her.

TOINETTE [*imitating him*] And I absolutely forbid her to do anything of the sort.

ARGAN [*shouts and waves the glass dangerously*] What are we coming to! What kind of insolence is this, for a rascally servant to talk that way in front of her master?

TOINETTE [*saves the glass from* ARGAN's *hand, reprovingly; puts it on medicine table*] When a master doesn't know what he's doing, it's the duty of a sensible servant to put him in the right way.

[*She has her back to* ARGAN.]

ARGAN [*rises, goes behind chair, takes his cane*] You insolent scoundrel, I'll have to teach you a lesson.

TOINETTE [*turns, sees* ARGAN, *utters a cry, runs to opposite side of chair from him. Provokingly*] It is my duty to prevent you from doing something which would dishonor you.

ARGAN [*moves around chair to reach her*] Come here, come here; I'll teach you how to talk.

TOINETTE [*circles around chair*] I am naturally interested in keeping you from doing something silly.

ARGAN [*pursues* TOINETTE *around chair, waving his stick*] Slut!

TOINETTE [*circles chair, runs behind bed*] No, I will never consent to this marriage.

ARGAN [*following her*] You she-devil!

TOINETTE [*circles bed, with* ARGAN *on opposite side*] I don't wish her to marry your Thomas Diafoirus.

ARGAN [*tries to hit* TOINETTE *across bed; falls flat on it*] Wench!

TOINETTE [*comes downstage behind* ANGÉLIQUE, *who has remained petrified in center*] She will obey me instead of you.

ARGAN [*stands up on bed*] Angélique, won't you stop that rascal there?

ANGÉLIQUE Oh, Father, don't make yourself ill again!

ARGAN If you don't stop her, I will put my parental curse on you.

TOINETTE And as for me, I will disinherit her if she obeys you.

[*Enter* BÉLINE. *She stops in surprise.* TOINETTE *and* ANGÉLIQUE *turn toward her, curtsey to her, and exit, one on each side.* ARGAN *collapses on bed and slides to floor.*]

ARGAN Oh, oh, oh, I'm done for. This will kill me. . . . Oh, oh, come here, darling.

BÉLINE [*going to him; in cajoling tone*] What's the matter, my poor dear?

ARGAN Come here and help me.

BÉLINE [*picks him up and helps him to sit on the platform at foot of bed*] What's the matter, my little boy?

ARGAN My darling!

BÉLINE My baby!

ARGAN They've been making me angry, precious.

BÉLINE Oh, my poor little lambie! How did they do that, my sweet?

ARGAN Your slut of a Toinette has become more insolent than ever.

BÉLINE Now don't get excited, my little pet.

ARGAN She put me in a rage, darling.

BÉLINE Calm down, baby; there, there.

ARGAN She went on for an hour interfering with the things I want to do.

BÉLINE There, there, just take things easy.

ARGAN And she had the impudence to tell me I am not sick.

    [*He begins to cough;* BÉLINE *draws back, with an involuntary quiver of disgust.*]

BÉLINE She's an impertinent hussy.

ARGAN You know, darling, that's not so. [*He coughs until he is out of breath.*]

BÉLINE Yes, dearest, she's quite wrong.

ARGAN [*continuing to cough*] Sweetheart, that wench will be the death of me.

BÉLINE [*pats* ARGAN'S *back*] There, there; there, there.

ARGAN [*draws a long whistling breath, stops coughing. He pats his stomach.*] She is the cause of all the bile I'm producing.

BÉLINE Don't get so excited, baby.

ARGAN And I've been telling you for I don't know how long to get rid of her.

BÉLINE [*becoming annoyed*] After all, darling, all servants have something wrong with them. You have to put up with their bad qualities on account of their good ones. Toinette knows her business and she's a good worker; and most of all she's trustworthy. And you know that nowadays you have to be very careful about the kind of people you take into your home. [ARGAN *mumbles, unconvinced.* BÉLINE *calls, turning her back on* ARGAN.] Oh, Toinette!

    [*Enter* TOINETTE, *wearing the sweetest of expressions.*]

TOINETTE Yes, ma'am?

BÉLINE Tell me, why did you make my husband angry?

TOINETTE Me, ma'am? Oh dear, I don't know what you mean. I always do my best to make him happy in every way.

ARGAN [*bounding in his chair*] Oh, the scamp!

[BÉLINE *soothes him.*]

TOINETTE He told us that he wanted to marry Angélique to the son of Dr. Diafoirus. I only said that I thought it would be a very good match for her, but I thought he would do better to put her in a convent.

BÉLINE [*turning to* ARGAN] There's nothing so bad about that. I rather think she is right.

ARGAN What, darling, you believe her? She's a villain; she was just as impudent as could be.

BÉLINE Of course, dearie, of course. There, there, calm down. [*Turns toward* TOINETTE.] Listen, Toinette. If you ever make my husband angry, I will discharge you. [TOINETTE *is about to protest.* BÉLINE *signals to her:* "Hush, it's just to satisfy him." TOINETTE *smiles broadly.*] There, give me his fur-lined gown. [*She rouses* ARGAN. TOINETTE *goes to the bed, takes gown, brings it back and puts it around* ARGAN's *shoulders.*] And some pillows. [TOINETTE *makes a pile of six pillows.* BÉLINE *helps* ARGAN *to his chair.*] I'll fix him up nicely in his little chair. You're all every which way, darling. [ARGAN *sits down, and sneezes.*] Pull down your little night-cap over your precious ears. The best way to catch a cold is through the ears.

ARGAN Oh, sweetheart, how grateful I am to you for all the good care you take of me!

[*During this speech,* TOINETTE *has come up with the pile of pillows.* BÉLINE *tries to take the top one, which is out of her reach.* TOINETTE *bends over, and rises up every time* BÉLINE *takes a pillow.*]

BÉLINE Get up a second, let me put this under you. Let's put this one here for you to rest your arm on . . . and this one on the other side. [*She passes around chair.*] And we'll put this one behind your back . . . and this one to support your sweet head.

TOINETTE And this one to protect you from the bad air!
[*She slaps the last pillow on his face, and runs out.*
BÉLINE *restrains her impulse to laugh.*]

ARGAN Oh, you rapscallion, you want to smother me to death!
[*He rises, furious, throws the last pillow into the wings, after* TOINETTE. *He takes the pillow from under his right arm and throws it savagely at the bed platform.*]

BÉLINE There, there; there, there! [*She goes to pick up the second pillow.* ARGAN *takes the pillow from under his left arm, throws it wildly—but it hits* BÉLINE's *back as she is bending over to pick up the second pillow.*] What's the matter with you anyway?
[*She picks up the third pillow.*]

ARGAN [*to avoid a scolding, sinks back in his chair*] Oh, dear, oh, dear, I'm all in!
[*Feeling a troublesome pillow beneath him, he pulls it out and throws it into the wings. He collapses in the chair.*]

BÉLINE [*returns to him, disposes around him the two pillows she is carrying*] Why do you get so angry? She thought she was being nice to you.

ARGAN Darling, you don't know how sly that little devil is. Oh, oh, she has put me in a terrible state. I'll need more than eight purges and a dozen enemas to make up for all this.

BÉLINE [*arranging* ARGAN's *nightcap*] There, there, my sweet, just calm down.

ARGAN My dearest, you are all my consolation in this world.

BÉLINE My poor baby!

ARGAN [*takes* BÉLINE's *hands, places them affectionately around his neck*] And just to show that I appreciate all your love for me, dearest, I want to make my will, as I've already told you.

BÉLINE [*coming beside chair*] Oh, darling, let's not talk

about that sort of thing, I beg you. I just can't bear such a thought, and if you merely mention the word "will," it makes me shudder all over.

ARGAN But didn't I tell you to speak to your notary about that?

BÉLINE [*pointing to rear*] I did bring him; he's right outside.

ARGAN Bring him in, my love.

BÉLINE Oh dear, my darling, when a girl loves her husband so much, she's in no condition to think about things like that.

[*She kisses* ARGAN *lightly on the brow, goes to rear steps. Music. The curtains open, disclosing the notary, bowing almost double. He straightens up, descends the steps, and bows again to the ground as music ceases.*]

ARGAN Come here, Monsieur de Bonnefoi, come here. [*The notary makes a third bow to* ARGAN.] Take a chair, won't you? [*The notary does so.*] My dear sir, my wife has told me that you are a very trustworthy man, and an excellent friend of hers. So I told her to speak to you about a will I am thinking of making.

BÉLINE [*goes beside* ARGAN. *He takes her hand.*] Oh, dear, I just can't talk about things like that.

BONNEFOI [*sharp and business-like*] Monsieur, she has explained to me your intentions and the purposes you have with regard to her. And I must tell you on that score that you cannot give anything to your wife by will.

ARGAN And why not?

BONNEFOI [*emphatic; categorical*] Common law forbids it. If we were in a region of statute law, it would be possible. But in Paris and in the areas of common law, or at least in most of them, that is not permitted, and such a disposition would be null and void. The only special provision that a man and woman conjoined by marriage can make one for the other is a mutual gift or donation *inter vivos,* while they are both alive. And even in that case it is stipulated that there must be no children, whether of the two conjoined, or of one separately, at the time of the decease of the first to so decede.

ARGAN That's a very unreasonable common law, it seems to me, if a husband can't leave anything to a wife who loves him tenderly and who takes such good care of him! [*Glances at* BÉLINE.] I would like to consult my lawyer to see if I can't do anything.

BONNEFOI [*reflecting whether something mightn't be done*] I shouldn't consult any lawyers on the subject, for they are ordinarily very particular about this sort of thing, and they think it's a great crime to make any dispositions which might get around the law. They're people who do nothing but make difficulties, and they pay no attention to the special cases and requirements of a man's conscience. But there are other people you can consult who are much more accommodating, who know the expedients for getting around the law and justifying what is not permitted in theory, and who can smooth out the difficulties of certain cases and find ways of slipping through the common law for some particular advantage. If it weren't for that, where would we all be? There has to be a certain facility in things; otherwise nothing would ever be accomplished, and our business wouldn't be worth a penny.

ARGAN In fact, my wife had told me, sir, that you were a very clever notary [BONNEFOI *bows*] and a very honest man. [BONNEFOI *bows again.*] Tell me, please, how I can give her my property and keep it out of the hands of my children?

BONNEFOI How you can do that? [*He rises, and, holding the chair to his seat, moves close to* ARGAN'*s chair. Conspiratorially.*] You can just pick out some close friend of your wife's, and duly give him in your will all that you can; and then this friend will give everything back to her. [*He looks at* BÉLINE; *she signals "No" with her finger.*] Or again, you can make out a large number of notes, all open and above-board, toward certain creditors, and they will make these over to your wife, and put a signed statement in her

hands that their procedure has been entirely for her con-
venience and pleasure. [*Same business with* BÉLINE.] Or
again, you can put actual cash in her hands while you are
still alive [*he glances at* BÉLINE, *who nods assent*] or notes
which you will make payable to bearer.

BÉLINE Oh, dear, you mustn't worry your head about
things like that. If you should ever go away and leave us,
my darling, I don't want to live another day.

ARGAN My sweet!

BÉLINE Yes, dearest, if I should be so unhappy as to lose
you—

ARGAN My own dear wife!

BÉLINE Life won't mean a thing to me.

ARGAN My love!

BÉLINE And I will follow you to the other world, just to
show how much I love you. [*She throws herself into* ARGAN'S
arms. Both weep.]

ARGAN Darling, you're breaking my heart. Cheer up,
please; cheer up.

BONNEFOI [*sniffling with sympathy*] There is no reason
for tears. Things haven't got to that point yet.

BÉLINE [*rising*] My dear sir, you don't know what it is
to have a husband you love with all your heart.

ARGAN If I die, darling, I have only one regret; it is that
I haven't got a child by you. But Dr. Purgon told me that he
would arrange it.

BONNEFOI Oh well, that may happen any time.

ARGAN [*shakes his head despondently, then decides to get
down to business*] I must make my will, darling, as this
gentleman has suggested. But just as a precaution I am going
to put in your hands twenty thousand francs in gold which
I have hidden behind the panelling, and two notes payable
to bearer which are due, one from Monsieur Damon, and
the other from Monsieur Géronte.

BÉLINE [*with a gesture of refusal*] No, I don't want any
of it at all. [*She returns toward him.*] How much did you
say there is behind the panelling?

ARGAN Twenty thousand francs, my love.

BÉLINE [*shuddering*] Don't talk about money, please. . . . How much are the two notes for?

ARGAN Darling, one is for four thousand francs, the other for six.

BÉLINE Sweetheart, all the money in the world is nothing to me in comparison with you.

[*She throws herself into his arms.* BONNEFOI *turns aside politely, and coughs to indicate his presence.*]

BONNEFOI Would you like to draft the will immediately?

ARGAN Yes, indeed, but we will be more comfortable in my study. [*He rises without aid, and suddenly remembers his illness.*] Darling, help me out, please.

BÉLINE Come, my poor little baby.

[*She takes his arm, and leads him toward exit. She gets* ARGAN *in front of her, takes a purse from her corsage and holds it out to* BONNEFOI. *He receives it, bowing deeply. Exit* ARGAN, BÉLINE, BONNEFOI.

[*Enter* TOINETTE *rapidly from opposite side. She crosses stage to exit where the three have gone out. She listens; runs back and fetches* ANGÉLIQUE, *pulling her onstage by the hand.*]

TOINETTE They are in there with the notary, and I heard them talking about a will. Your stepmother has all her wits about her. I'll bet she is getting your father into some kind of plot against your interests.

ANGÉLIQUE Let him dispose of his property as he pleases, provided he does not dispose of my heart. Toinette, you can see how they are leading him around by the nose. Don't abandon me, dear, in this awful situation.

TOINETTE Would I abandon you? I'd rather die. It's no use if your stepmother does play up to me and try to get me tangled up in her plans, I never could stand her, and I've always been on your side. Just leave it to me; I'll do everything to help you out. But if I'm really going to help you out, I'd better not come into the open. I'd better pretend to agree with your father and your stepmother.

ANGÉLIQUE Only try to let Cléante know about the marriage that has been arranged.

BÉLINE [*offstage*] Toinette!

TOINETTE She's calling me. Good-bye. [*She goes to exit; turns back to* ANGÉLIQUE.] Trust in me!

[*Exit.* ANGÉLIQUE *sighs.*]

CURTAIN

FIRST ENTR'ACTE

[*This interlude, a carnival scene with dance and song, has nothing to do with the plot of the play, and is therefore omitted.*]

ACT II

[*The scene is unchanged. Musical overture. The curtain rises on an empty stage. Musical theme for* CLÉANTE. *Curtains at rear open, disclosing* CLÉANTE *motionless, facing audience. He descends steps, advances downstage, surveys room with interest. Enter* TOINETTE. *She does not recognize him; shows surprise.*]

TOINETTE What do you want here, sir?

CLÉANTE [*turns toward her*] What do I want?

TOINETTE Aha, it's you! What a surprise! But what are you doing here?

[*Both talk hastily and confidentially, in fear of surprise.*]

CLÉANTE I have come to learn my fate, to speak to my lovely Angélique, to discover the state of her feelings, and to ask her what she plans to do about that appalling engagement which has been reported to me.

TOINETTE Yes, but you won't have a chance to talk things over openly with Angélique. You know how carefully they watch over her; they won't let her go out or talk to anyone; and the only reason we were allowed to go to the play where your little romance began was because her old aunt was so crazy to see the show. And naturally we have been very careful not to talk about that adventure.

CLÉANTE I know. And that's why I have not come here today as her suitor Cléante. I have come as a friend of her music teacher. He has given me permission to say that I'm replacing him.

TOINETTE Here's her father. You go out for a minute, and let me tell him you're here.

[*She pulls him offstage, and exits after him. Enter* ARGAN. *He is about to take a walk for exercise. He halts, his leg and cane in mid-air.*]

ARGAN Dr. Purgon told me to walk twelve times across my room in the morning, but I forgot to ask him whether he meant the long way or the short way.

[*He makes up his mind, starts again. Enter* TOINETTE *hurriedly.*]

TOINETTE Monsieur, there's a man here . . .

ARGAN Don't talk so loud, you slut! You get my brains all rattled, and you never seem to realize that you mustn't talk so loud to invalids.

TOINETTE I just wanted to tell you, sir . . .

ARGAN [*walking with concentration*] Don't talk so loud, I tell you.

[*He walks to side of stage, turns, obviously keeping count.*]

TOINETTE [*joins him as he walks, speaks confidentially into his ear*] Monsieur . . .

ARGAN [*stops, center, cranes his head toward her*] What's that?

TOINETTE I'm trying to tell you . . .

ARGAN What are you saying?

TOINETTE [*shouting in his ear*] I'm saying there's a man here who wants to speak to you.

ARGAN [*putting his hands over his ears*] Tell him to come in.

[*He resumes his walk, counting his trips.* TOINETTE *signals to* CLÉANTE *to enter.* ARGAN *continues his walk to the wings, turns, and makes the return trip solemnly. Enter* CLÉANTE.]

CLÉANTE [*loudly, with determination*] Sir . . . [ARGAN *halts.*]

TOINETTE [*runs to* CLÉANTE'S *side, her finger on lips*] Don't talk so loud, or you'll make his brains rattle.

[CLÉANTE *is bewildered.* ARGAN *resumes his promenade.*]

CLÉANTE [*ingratiatingly*] Sir, I am delighted to find that you are up and to see that your health is better.

[ARGAN *stops, annoyed.*]

TOINETTE What do you mean, his health is better? That's not true. Monsieur is always sick.

[ARGAN *smiles, resumes his promenade.*]

CLÉANTE [*uncomprehending*] I had heard that Monsieur was better, and I think he is looking very well.

TOINETTE What do you mean, he's looking very well? He's looking very badly, and anyone who says he's looking better is crazy. He's never been so sick.

ARGAN She's quite right.

TOINETTE He walks, sleeps, eats and drinks like anybody else. But that doesn't keep him from being very sick.

ARGAN That's very true.

CLÉANTE [*getting the idea, and joining* ARGAN *on his trips to and fro*] Sir, I am shocked indeed to hear it. I have been sent by your daughter's singing teacher. He has had to go to the country for a few days, and since I'm his good friend, he sent me in his place to continue her lessons, so that she won't have to interrupt them and forget everything she has learned.

ARGAN Very well. Call Angélique.

TOINETTE [*joining* ARGAN] I think, sir, it would be better to take this gentleman to her room.

ARGAN No, bring her here.

TOINETTE [*after exchange of glances with* CLÉANTE] He won't be able to give her a proper lesson unless they're alone.

ARGAN Yes he will, yes he will.

TOINETTE [*planting herself before* ARGAN *and checking his promenade*] Monsieur, that will just upset you, and the slightest thing is enough to distress you in your present state, and rattle your brains.

ARGAN No, no, not at all; I like music, and I would be very glad to . . . [*Enter* ANGÉLIQUE. CLÉANTE *turns his back to her. Seeing a stranger, she stops.*] Ah, here she is. [*To* TOINETTE.] You go and see if my wife is dressed yet. [*Exit* TOINETTE. ARGAN *goes to* ANGÉLIQUE, *takes her hand, leads her downstage.* CLÉANTE *turns to her and bows deeply, so that she sees only his peruke.*] Come, my dear; your music teacher has gone to the country, and here's a person he has sent in his place to give you your lesson.

[*He drops her hand and prepares to resume his consti-*

tutional. He has his back to the pair. CLÉANTE *stands
upright.*]

ANGÉLIQUE Good heavens!

ARGAN [*turning around*] What's the matter? Why are you
surprised?

ANGÉLIQUE It's . . .

ARGAN What? What upsets you so?

ANGÉLIQUE Father, this is really a surprising thing.

ARGAN What do you mean?

ANGÉLIQUE I dreamt last night that I was in some dreadful
trouble, and a man who looked just like this gentleman here
presented himself [ARGAN *looks suspiciously at* CLÉANTE]
and I asked him for help, and he rescued me from all the
trouble I was in. So I was much surprised to see here un-
expectedly just what I had the idea of last night.

CLÉANTE One must regard himself as fortunate who can
occupy your thoughts, whether you are asleep or awake.
Certainly I should be very happy if you should be in some
trouble from which you would judge me worthy of rescuing
you; and there is nothing I would not do to . . .

[*Enter* TOINETTE, *running and talking. She takes*
ARGAN's *arm. During her speech, she and* ARGAN *survey
his clothing, to make sure he is presentable. Meanwhile*
CLÉANTE *seizes the occasion to kiss* ANGÉLIQUE's *hands.*]

TOINETTE To tell you the truth, sir, now I'm on your
side, and I take back everything I said yesterday. Here is
Dr. Diafoirus the father and Dr. Diafoirus the son; they've
come to pay you a visit. What a son-in-law you are going to
have! You are going to see the finest-looking young fellow on
earth, and so bright! He only said two words, but those were
so well said! Your daughter is going to be charmed with him.

ARGAN [*turns around;* CLÉANTE *springs away from* ANGÉ-
LIQUE. *To* CLÉANTE, *thinking* CLÉANTE *is taking his leave*]
Don't go away, Monsieur. The fact is, I am having my
daughter married, and now they are bringing her future
husband here, whom she hasn't yet seen.

CLÉANTE You honor me very much, sir, to wish me to be a witness of such a delightful interview.

ARGAN He's the son of a very good doctor, and the marriage will take place in four days.

CLÉANTE Very fine.

ARGAN You let her music teacher know about it, and tell him to come to the wedding.

CLÉANTE I won't fail to. -

ARGAN You come too.

CLÉANTE You do me too much honor.

TOINETTE Now everybody get ready. Here they are.

[*Music. The curtains, rear, are opened, revealing the* DIAFOIRUSES, *father and son, posing.* THOMAS *has an enormous roll of parchment, his thesis, under his arm. Accompanied by his musical motif,* DR. DIAFOIRUS *advances majestically. To his motif,* THOMAS *trots forward to join him. They bow in unison, as music ceases. Curtains at rear remain open.*]

ARGAN [*bows*] Sir, Dr. Purgon has forbidden me to bare my head. You, as a member of the profession, know what the consequences would be.

DIAFOIRUS Sir, it is our constant concern to bring aid to the ill, and never to jeopardize their health.

ARGAN I accept, sir . . .

DIAFOIRUS We have come here, sir . . .

ARGAN With much joy . . .

DIAFOIRUS My son Thomas and I . . .

ARGAN The honor you do me . . .

DIAFOIRUS To testify to you, sir . . .

ARGAN And I would have dearly liked . . .

DIAFOIRUS The pleasure which is ours . . .

ARGAN To be able to call at your home . . .

DIAFOIRUS At the honor you do us . . .

ARGAN To assure you of my pleasure . . .

DIAFOIRUS In receiving us so honorably . . .

ARGAN But you know, sir . . .

DIAFOIRUS Into the honor, sir . . .

ARGAN What a poor invalid is . . .

DIAFOIRUS Of an alliance with you . . .

ARGAN Who can do nothing else . . .

DIAFOIRUS And to assure you . . .

ARGAN Than to tell you now . . .

DIAFOIRUS That in every matter relating to our profession . . .

ARGAN That I will seek every occasion . . .

DIAFOIRUS As in every other matter . . .

ARGAN To make evident to you . . .

DIAFOIRUS We shall always be ready, sir . . .

ARGAN That I am entirely at your service . . .

DIAFOIRUS To testify to you our zeal and good will.

[*In the stage version, these speeches may be otherwise grouped, to make them intelligible to the audience. The two begin ceremoniously, then talk louder and more impatiently. The last three pairs of speeches are made simultaneously, each speaker shouting at the top of his lungs.*]

DIAFOIRUS [*out of breath*] Come here, Thomas. Pay your compliments.

THOMAS [*steps forward, hesitates, turns back to his father. In a high, bleating voice*] Don't I begin with the father?

DIAFOIRUS Yes.

THOMAS [*takes his stand before ARGAN, throws his head back, shuts his eyes, and recites a painfully memorized speech*] Sir, I come to salute recognize cherish and revere in you a second father but a second father to whom if I may say so I am more deeply indebted than to my first father. The first father gave me birth but you have freely chosen me. He received me through necessity but you have accepted me through your good grace. What I have from him is a work of the body but what I have from you is a work of the will, and just as much as the spiritual faculties are superior to the corporeal so much the more am I indebted to you and so much the more do I hold precious this future filial relationship for which I come to you today to render you in advance my most humble and most respectful homage.

> [*He smiles with great satisfaction at his father.* DIAFOIRUS, *who has been muttering the same speech with his lips, smiles broadly in return.*]

TOINETTE Hurrah for the colleges which produce such brilliant men!

THOMAS [*confidentially*] Was it all right, Father?

DIAFOIRUS *Optime.*

ARGAN [*to* ANGÉLIQUE] Come, salute the young gentleman.

> [ANGÉLIQUE *drops a deep curtsey.*]

THOMAS [*replies with an awkward bob of the knees. To his father*] Do I kiss?

DIAFOIRUS Yes, yes.

THOMAS [*happily approaches* ANGÉLIQUE, *to kiss her forehead. She avoids the kiss by making another curtsey, and nearly upsets* THOMAS. ARGAN *intervenes between the two.*] Madame, it is with justice that heaven has bestowed upon you the title of stepmother, since . . .

> [TOINETTE *bursts out laughing.*]

ARGAN That isn't my wife, it's my daughter you're talking to.

THOMAS Where is your wife?

ARGAN She is coming.

THOMAS [*returns to his father*] Do I wait for her to come?

DIAFOIRUS [*annoyed at his son's error*] Go ahead and make Mademoiselle's compliment.

THOMAS [*takes ceremonious stand before* ANGÉLIQUE. *His speech is almost a chant, without emphasis. Dr. Diafoirus accompanies his speech with movements of the lips.*] Mademoiselle, just as the statue of Memnon rendered forth a harmonious sound when it was first lit by the rays of the sun so do I feel myself animated by sweet transport at the appearance of the sun of your beauty. And as naturalists have observed that the flower called heliotrope turns incessantly toward that orb of day so will my heart henceforce turn always toward the resplendent orbs of your adorable eyes as towards its only pole. [*His memory fails him; he repeats "only pole" desperately. His father prompts him: "Permit me." THOMAS smiles gratefully and resumes.*] Permit me therefore mademoiselle to hang upon the altar of your charms the offering of this heart [*gesture toward heart*] which breathes and aspires to no other glory than to be all its life mademoiselle your most humble most obedient and most faithful servant and husband.

[*He returns to his father's side and is congratulated in dumbshow.*]

TOINETTE That's what education does; you learn to say such beautiful things.

ARGAN [*To* CLÉANTE] Well! What do you say to that?

CLÉANTE I should say that the gentleman does marvellously well. If he's as good a doctor as he is a public speaker, it would be a pleasure to be one of his patients.

TOINETTE Yes indeed. It will be wonderful, if he cures as well as he talks.

ARGAN Come now, quick, my chair, and seats for everybody.

[TOINETTE *disposes the chairs. She pushes forward* ARGAN's *easy chair; he posts himself in front of it. She puts a stool beside it;* DIAFOIRUS *takes his place before it.* ARGAN *was preparing to sit; he straightens up and mimics to* DIAFOIRUS: "*After you.*" DIAFOIRUS *starts to sit, then straightens, gesturing to* ARGAN: "*After you.*" *After some byplay, the two succeed in sitting down together. Meanwhile,* TOINETTE *has placed a stool for* THOMAS. *As he is about to sit,* TOINETTE *utters a little scream. He starts up, frightened.*]

ARGAN You sit down there, my dear daughter. [*He points to* THOMAS' *stool.* ANGÉLIQUE *crosses, prepares to sit.* THOMAS *looks for a place to sit.* ARGAN *signals to* TOINETTE *to fetch him a chair. She exits, as* CLÉANTE *takes his seat. To* DIAFOIRUS] You see, sir, that everyone admires your son, and I am very happy to find him such a fine fellow.

[TOINETTE *returns with a child's high chair and places
it beside* ANGÉLIQUE'S *stool.* THOMAS *struggles to insert
himself in it, finally succeeds.*]

DIAFOIRUS [*speaks when everyone is seated. During his
speech* ARGAN *dozes,* THOMAS *attempts to cajole* ANGÉLIQUE,
CLÉANTE *watches with an angry air.*] Sir, if I may attempt
to speak without paternal prejudice, I may say that I have
every reason to be well satisfied with him. All who know
him agree that there is not an ounce of wickedness in him.
He has never had a very lively imagination, nor that fiery
nature which is so common, but for that very reason I have
always augured well of his judgment, the quality most requisite for the exercise of our art. When he was small, he was
never mischievous and troublesome. He was always quiet
and well behaved, he never said a word, and he never played
at those games known as juvenile. We had all sorts of trouble
teaching him to read, and when he was nine years old he
didn't yet know his letters. "Good," I said to myself, "slow-
growing trees are the ones which produce the best fruit. It
is harder to engrave upon marble than upon sand, but what
is inscribed thereon lasts much longer; and this slowness of
comprehension, this heaviness of imagination, is the mark
of a good judgment to come." When I sent him to school,
he had indeed some trouble; but he reacted against all the
difficulties, and his teachers reported most favorably on his
persistence and his industry. Finally, by everlastingly stick-
ing to it, he succeeded in getting his degrees most creditably;
and I may say without vanity that during the last two years,
when he has been working for the final degree, no candidate
has made more noise than he in all the school discussions.
He has become really formidable; whenever any proposition
is brought up he will argue to the bitter end for the opposite
side. He is firm in dispute, obstinate as a mule on his principles, he never alters his opinion, and he follows a line of
reasoning to the last confines of logic. But above all what
I like in him is that, following my own example, he accepts
without question the opinions of the great ancients, and he

has always refused to listen for a moment to the arguments and experiments concerning the alleged discoveries of our own time with regard to the circulation of the blood and similar nonsense.

THOMAS [*extricating himself from his chair*] I have written a thesis against the believers in the circulation of the blood, and if Monsieur Argan will permit me, I may venture to present it to Mademoiselle as a fitting homage of the first-fruits of my achievement.

[*He proudly lays the great roll on her knees.*]

ANGÉLIQUE Sir, I really don't know what to do with it; I am no judge of such matters.

TOINETTE Give it to me; maybe there's a picture in it; we could put it on the wall.

[*She takes the roll and throws it on the bed.*]

THOMAS If Monsieur Argan will permit, I should like to invite you, for your entertainment, to come and see the dissection of a woman, which I am to demonstrate.

TOINETTE That will be a delightful entertainment. Some suitors put on a play for their fiancées, but to put on a dissection would be much more genteel.

DIAFOIRUS [*beckons* ARGAN *to him; confidentially*] Besides, as for the qualities requisite for marriage and propagation, I may assure you that, according to the rules of medicine, he is all that could be wished. He possesses the prolific virtue to a laudable degree, and he is of the proper temperament to engender and procreate well-conditioned children.

[*Mutual gesture of understanding.* THOMAS, *who has overheard, coughs complacently.*]

ARGAN [*in an offhand manner, disguising his real concern*] Is it not your intention, sir, to push him at court and to establish him as a court physician?

DIAFOIRUS To speak frankly, I have never cared for the practice of our profession among the nobles; I have always thought that we do much better to practise with the general public. The public treats you properly. You don't have to justify your actions to anyone; if you merely follow the rules of our art, you have no trouble about anything that may happen. But the annoying thing about dealing with the nobles is that when they fall ill they absolutely demand that their doctors cure them.

TOINETTE How absurd! They are certainly unreasonable to expect that you gentlemen should *cure* them! That's not what you're there for. Your job is to prescribe the remedies, for your fees; it's up to them to get well, if they can.

DIAFOIRUS Quite right. We are required only to treat patients according to the proper forms.

[THOMAS *laughs a giggling laugh.* DIAFOIRUS *reproves him with a glance. An awkward moment.*]

ARGAN [*to* CLÉANTE, *to clear the air*] Sir, won't you have my daughter sing something to the company?

CLÉANTE [*rises and advances*] I was expecting such an order, sir, and it occurred to me that I might divert the company by singing with mademoiselle a scene from an opera which has just appeared. [*Bows to* ANGÉLIQUE.] Here is your part.

[*Offers her a sheet of music.*]

ANGÉLIQUE Me?

[*She rises and takes the music.*]

CLÉANTE [*takes* ANGÉLIQUE *by the hand, leads her to the bed platform, stations her on it, while making an aside to her.*] Don't refuse, please, and let me tell you what the scene is that we're going to sing. [*To the assembled group.*] I really haven't a singing voice, but it's enough if I carry the meaning, and you will be kind enough to excuse me, so that you may hear mademoiselle sing.

ARGAN It's poetry?

CLÉANTE It's really a little impromptu opera, and you will hear only prose in cadence, or a sort of free verse, such as emotion and the circumstances may inspire in people who are saying things naturally and are speaking without preparation.

ARGAN All right. Let's hear it.

CLÉANTE [*after a moment's hesitation*] Here is the subject

of the scene. A shepherd was watching some performance
which was beginning, when he was distracted by a noise
near him. He turns around, and he sees a brutal fellow in-
sulting a shepherdess with insolent words. He comes to her
rescue; and after giving the brute a proper punishment, he
goes to the shepherdess whose tears—beautiful tears—[*he
turns toward* ANGÉLIQUE] were falling from the most beautiful eyes he had ever seen. [*He turns back to the family.*]
"Alas!" he says to himself, "how can anyone outrage so lovely
a person? What human being, nay what barbarian, would
not be moved by such distress?" He does his best to dry
those tears which he finds so beautiful; and the lovely shepherdess tries to thank him for the slight service he has
rendered her, but in such a charming manner, so tender, so
heartfelt [*he turns toward* ANGÉLIQUE] that the shepherd
cannot resist, and every word, every glance, is a flaming shaft
which seems to pierce his heart. [*He is forgetting his public;
he comes to himself and turns toward them.*] He says to
himself: "Is there anything which can merit such delightful
thanks? What wouldn't one do, what dangers would one not
gladly risk, to gain for a moment the touching effusions of
this grateful heart?" So the spectacle they were watching
continues, but he pays no attention to it. He complains only
that it is too short, because when it is over he must separate
from his adorable shepherdess. And from this first sight, this
first moment, he is smitten by a love so intense that it seems
the product of years of devotion. He feels all the sufferings
of absence; he is tortured because he sees her no more. He
tries his best to have access to her [*he turns toward* ANGÉ-
LIQUE], but she is so closely guarded that he finds no means.
He resolves to ask the hand in marriage of this adorable
creature without whom he can no longer live, and he asks
her permission to pay his suit, in a letter which he gets into
her hands; and she grants her permission. [ARGAN *nods ap-
provingly.*] But at the same time he is warned that the
father of this lovely girl has arranged her marriage with
another, and that they are preparing to proceed with the

ceremony. You may imagine how the unhappy shepherd
suffers. He cannot bear the appalling thought of seeing his
beloved in another's arms, and his desperate love discovers
a way to get into the house of his shepherdess [*he turns
toward* ANGÉLIQUE] to learn the state of her feelings and
to find from her the fate to which he must resign himself.
[*Turns back to the group; addresses* THOMAS.] He finds there
all in preparation for what he most fears; he sees there the
unworthy rival whom the caprice of a father is opposing to
the tenderness of his love. He sees this ridiculous rival
triumphant, in the presence of the lovely shepherdess, as if
she were an assured conquest, and this sight fills him with
anger which he can hardly control. [*He turns to* ANGÉ-
LIQUE.] He looks with grief on his adored one, but the
presence of her father, and respect for him, prevent him
from speaking, except with his eyes. [*He turns toward the
two fathers.*] But finally he overcomes all his constraint, and
the transport of his love obliges him to speak to her, thus
[*He leaps on the bed platform, beside* ANGÉLIQUE, *who un-
rolls her music. Sings*]:

> Fair Phyllis, I've suffered, I've suffered too
>   long;
> An end to your silence, and answer my song!
> And tell me what fate, what fortune have I:
>   To live or to die?

ANGÉLIQUE You see me, Tircis, sorrowful, despairing,
> Watching the wedding others are preparing.
> I look to Heaven, and look at you, and sigh;
>   What other course have I?

ARGAN [*much pleased, to* DIAFOIRUS] Well, well! I didn't
know my daughter could sing so well at sight without
hesitating.

CLÉANTE Alas, fair Phyllis,
> Can it be true that ardent Tircis
> May have a share of rapture for his part
> And hold a little place within your heart?

ANGÉLIQUE What can I say in midst of my distress?
            Tircis, I love you, I confess.
CLÉANTE   Oh what a glorious revelation!
            Could I have made a misinterpretation?
            Dear Phyllis, make again your declaration!
ANGÉLIQUE Yes, Tircis, I love you.
CLÉANTE   Again, again!
ANGÉLIQUE I love you.
CLÉANTE   Begin again a hundred times, and never weary
               of it.
ANGÉLIQUE I love you, I love you,
            Yes, Tircis, I love you.

CLÉANTE [*facing the family group*]:

      Oh gods, oh kings, who see the world beneath
          your feet,
      Can you compare your happiness to mine?
      But Phyllis, there's a thought that comes to me
         To trouble all my joy—
         A rival, a rival . . .

ANGÉLIQUE [*to the family group*]:

      Oh, I hate him worse than death;
      Even his presence tortures me
      E'en as it tortures you.
CLÉANTE   What of the father's cruel commands?
         He bids you to comply.

ANGÉLIQUE [*to* CLÉANTE]:

      Ah no, I'd rather die!
      I never will comply!
      I'd rather, rather die, I'd rather die!

ARGAN And what does the father say to all this?
CLÉANTE [*in his rapture, takes a moment to understand*
ARGAN's *question*] He doesn't say anything.
    [*Impatiently, he turns again toward* ANGÉLIQUE, *prepares to sing.*]

ARGAN That father is a fool, to let such nonsense go on without saying a thing.

CLÉANTE [*has paid no attention to* ARGAN. *He gives* ARGAN *a hasty, polite smile, turns to* ANGÉLIQUE. *Sings*] Ah, my love . . .

ARGAN No, no, that's enough of that. That play gives a very bad example. That shepherd Tircis is a very impudent fellow, and the shepherdess Phyllis is impertinent to talk that way in front of her father. Show me that paper. [ANGÉLIQUE *reluctantly hands the music to* ARGAN. *He turns it over, up and down.*] Aha! Where are the words you sang? There's nothing written here but the music!

CLÉANTE [*comes downstage, faces* ARGAN] Didn't you know, sir, that we now have a way of writing the words with the notes themselves?

ARGAN All right. Very good. I am at your service, sir. And good-bye. [*He hands the music to* CLÉANTE. CLÉANTE *picks up his hat from his chair, bows to the assembly, and starts for rear exit.*] We could have well done without your idiotic opera.

CLÉANTE [*turning around*] I thought it would amuse you, sir.

ARGAN Nonsense is not amusing. [CLÉANTE *bows profoundly, exits, rear, with dignity. The curtains are drawn after him. A chilly moment.* ARGAN *sees* BÉLINE *entering. This is a relief.*] Ah, here's my wife.

[*Enter* BÉLINE. *All rise, except* THOMAS, *who has enjoyed* CLÉANTE's *song, and is still following him with his eyes.* ARGAN *goes to meet* BÉLINE, *brings her back by the hand.* DIAFOIRUS *bows,* BÉLINE *curtseys.* ANGÉLIQUE *withdraws to side of stage.*]

ARGAN My love, here is the son of Dr. Diafoirus.

[DIAFOIRUS *turns toward* THOMAS, *still seated, looking backward, absorbed; gives him a sharp blow on the shins with his cane.* THOMAS *turns his body, falls out of high chair, takes his stand before* BÉLINE, *makes a hasty bow, begins his singsong compliment.*]

THOMAS Madame, it is with justice that Heaven has bestowed upon you the title of stepmother, since it has taken steps . . .

BÉLINE Monsieur, I am delighted to have come here in time to have the honor to see you.

THOMAS Since it has taken steps . . . [DIAFOIRUS *prompts him, but he does not hear.*] Since it has taken steps . . . Madame, you interrupted me in the middle of my speech, and that has upset my memory.

DIAFOIRUS Thomas, save that for another time.

[THOMAS, *crestfallen, joins his father, who scolds him in dumbshow.*]

ARGAN [*to dissipate the chill; to* BÉLINE] My dear, I wish you had been here earlier.

TOINETTE Oh madame, you certainly missed it, about the second father, the statue of Memnon, and the flower called heliotrope.

[*She brings* ANGÉLIQUE's *chair cross-stage to* BÉLINE. DIAFOIRUS *is mollified by her compliments.* BÉLINE *sits, as do* ARGAN *and* DIAFOIRUS. *A moment's pause.*]

ARGAN [*to* ANGÉLIQUE] Come, my dear, take the young gentleman's hand and pledge him as your husband.

[THOMAS, *beaming, holds out his hand to* ANGÉLIQUE.]

ANGÉLIQUE [*hesitates, makes up her mind. Protesting*] Father!

ARGAN [*surprised and offended*] What's that, "Father"? What do you mean by that?

ANGÉLIQUE Father, please, don't hurry things. Give us at least time to get acquainted with each other, so that we can develop that natural inclination which is necessary for a perfect union.

THOMAS As for me, Mademoiselle, it has already developed in me, and I don't need to wait any longer.

ANGÉLIQUE [*as politely as possible*] If you are so quick, sir, it isn't the same with me, and I admit to you that your merits have not yet made a sufficient impression on my spirit.

ARGAN [*somewhat reassured*] Oh well, if that's all! Your inclination will have plenty of time to develop when you're married.

[*He laughs, to make the unpleasantness pass off.* DIA-
FOIRUS *responds with a laugh.*]

ANGÉLIQUE [*protesting*] Look, Father—give me time, I beg of you. [*Catches herself, becomes amiable.*] Marriage is a bond to which a heart should never be submitted by force. [*Pleading, to* THOMAS.] And if Monsieur is a gentleman, he should be unwilling to accept a person who is given to him under constraint.

THOMAS [*taking a chair and placing it in front of him, as if he were in a pulpit*] Nego consequentiam, I deny the consequence, Mademoiselle, and I can be a gentleman and still be willing to accept you from the hands of your honored father.

ANGÉLIQUE It's a poor way to gain someone's love, by persecuting her.

THOMAS [*climbs on bottom rung of chair, raises his fore-finger. Oratorically*] We read in the ancients, Mademoiselle, that it was their custom to carry off marriageable girls by force from their fathers' homes, so that it would appear that it was not by their own consent that they were received into a husband's arms.

ANGÉLIQUE [*sharply*] The ancients, sir, were ancients, and we are people of today. Such affectations are not neces-sary in our time, and when a marriage is pleasing to us, we are perfectly able to go to it without being dragged. [*Tries to be cajoling.*] Just be patient; if you love me, sir, you should wish everything that I wish.

THOMAS Yes, Mademoiselle, but up to and exclusive of the interests of my love.

ANGÉLIQUE But the great mark of love is that one submits oneself to the wishes of the person one loves.

THOMAS [*climbs on second rung of chair*] Distinguo, Mademoiselle; in all that does not concern the possession of the loved one, *concedo,* I grant it. But in what does regard that possession, *nego,* I deny it.

[*As* ANGÉLIQUE *is about to reply sharply,* TOINETTE *intervenes, to indicate a wiser course.* THOMAS *descends carefully from his perch.*]

TOINETTE [*to* ANGÉLIQUE] There's no use your arguing. The young gentleman is fresh out of college, and he'll always come out ahead of you. Why do you resist so much and refuse the glory of being associated with the noble Faculty of Medicine?

BÉLINE [*who has been facing the audience, with an air of disgust, speaks sharply, without turning her head*] Perhaps she has some other little fancy in mind.

ANGÉLIQUE [*exploding*] If I did have, Madame, it would be an entirely reasonable and proper one.

ARGAN [*more annoyed than angry*] Phoo! This certainly puts me in a nice position.

BÉLINE [*calming him*] If I were you, my darling, I wouldn't force her to marry. I know very well what I would do.

ANGÉLIQUE [*to* BÉLINE] I know what you mean, Madame, and I know all your kindness toward me. But perhaps your excellent advice will not be put into execution.

BÉLINE The fact is that nice, well brought up girls like you care nothing about obeying their fathers' wills and wishes. It was different in the old days.

ANGÉLIQUE The duty of a daughter has its limits, Madame; and according to both reason and the law her duty doesn't include everything.

BÉLINE That must mean that you're thinking about marriage, but you want to pick a husband according to your own fancy.

ANGÉLIQUE [*angrily, losing control of her prudence*] If my father won't give me a husband I like, at least I will beg him not to force me to marry one I can't love.

[*General shock.* THOMAS *is revolted. After a stupefied*

moment, DIAFOIRUS *rises, full of dignity, joins* THOMAS. *The two start toward rear exit.*]

ARGAN [*rises, joins the* DIAFOIRUSES *at foot of rear steps, to restrain them*] Gentlemen, I beg your pardon for all this.

ANGÉLIQUE [*a little overawed by events, looks to* TOINETTE *for help, and encounters the hard glance of* BÉLINE] Everyone has his own purposes in getting married. As for me, I want a husband I can truly love, to whom I can give all my affection for life, and I want to take proper precautions. There are some girls who take a husband only to escape from the repression of their parents, in order to be free to do what they want. There are others, Madame, who make of marriage a mere matter of self-interest; they only marry to get marriage-settlements, to get rich by the death of their husbands, and they run without scruple from husband to husband in order to get hold of their legacies. [BÉLINE *turns sharply to* ANGÉLIQUE *to answer, but* ANGÉLIQUE *continues.*] Those persons, truly enough, are not at all particular, and they are little concerned about the individual they marry.

BÉLINE [*rises in anger;* ANGÉLIQUE *remains calm*] You seem to be full of ideas today. I would like to know what you mean by all that.

ANGÉLIQUE [*innocently*] I, Madame? What could I mean, except what I say?

BÉLINE You're so stupid, my dear, that you're really unendurable.

[*Shrugs her shoulders and turns away, toward audience.*]

ANGÉLIQUE I know, Madame, you'd like to get me to say something out of order; but I warn you, you won't have that advantage.

BÉLINE [*to* ANGÉLIQUE] I never heard such insolence.

ANGÉLIQUE It's no use, Madame.

BÉLINE And you have such a ridiculous pride, such an absurd presumption, that everybody washes his hands of you.

[*Turns back toward audience.* THOMAS *shrugs his shoulders sympathetically.*]

ANGÉLIQUE Madame, all this won't help you at all; you

can't make me lose my temper. And to deprive you of all hope of succeeding in your purposes, I shall remove myself from your presence.

[*She curtseys to* BÉLINE, *comes downstage, and, with her back to the audience, drops a deep curtsey to the* DIAFOIRUSES, *who reply with a short nod. She starts for side exit.*]

ARGAN [*joins* ANGÉLIQUE *near exit*] Look, you've got to make up your mind one way or the other. Either you marry the young gentleman within four days or—into a convent. [ANGÉLIQUE, *stony-faced, exits. To* BÉLINE, *in soothing tone*] Don't you worry, my dear. I'll bring her round.

BÉLINE [*unnerved*] I am sorry to leave you, darling, but I have an important errand in town. I will be back soon.

ARGAN [*confidentially*] That's all right, my love. And stop in at your notary's and tell him to send on that little—you know.

[*Kisses her hand.* BÉLINE *moves toward side exit, curtseying to the* DIAFOIRUSES. *They bow deeply.*]

BÉLINE [*turning toward* ARGAN] Good-bye, my sweet.

ARGAN [*springs to* BÉLINE, *kisses her hands lingeringly*] Good-bye, my beautiful. [*Exit* BÉLINE. ARGAN *stares after her, blows her a kiss, turns back to the* DIAFOIRUSES.] There's a woman who loves me so—well, you can hardly believe it.

DIAFOIRUS Sir, we must now take leave of you.

ARGAN First, sir, I beg you just to tell me how I look to you.

[*Sits in his easy chair.*]

DIAFOIRUS [*goes to his side, pulls out his watch, takes* ARGAN'S *pulse, beckons to* THOMAS] Come, Thomas, take the gentleman's other wrist, to see if you can make a proper judgment about his pulse. [THOMAS *comes to other side of chair, pulls out watch, imitates his father's actions;* ARGAN'S *two arms are held aloft.*] Quid dicis?

THOMAS Dico that the gentleman's pulse is the pulse of a man who is not well.

DIAFOIRUS Good.

THOMAS It is a little bit hardish; one might even say hard.

DIAFOIRUS Excellent.

THOMAS Throbbing.

DIAFOIRUS *Bene.*

THOMAS Even a little fluttering.

DIAFOIRUS *Optime.*

THOMAS Which indicates a disorder in the splenic parenchyma, which is to say the spleen.

DIAFOIRUS Very good.

ARGAN [*pulls away his arms and crosses them defensively on his chest*] No; Dr. Purgon says it's my liver that's out of order.

DIAFOIRUS [*returning his watch to his pocket, as does* THOMAS] Oh well, when you say parenchyma you mean both, because of their close relationship, by means of the *vas breve,* the *pylorus,* and often the *choledochic meatuses.* No doubt he orders you to eat a lot of roast meat.

ARGAN No, nothing but boiled meat.

DIAFOIRUS Oh well, roast meat, boiled meat, all the same. He is prescribing very well for you; you couldn't be in better hands.

[*He bows, moves toward rear entrance. Curtains open.* THOMAS, *following his father, notices* TOINETTE, *is much taken by her. She holds out her hand; he feels her pulse.*]

ARGAN [*rises to reconduct* DIAFOIRUS, *stopping the latter as he is mounting the steps*] Doctor, how many grains of salt should I put on an egg?

DIAFOIRUS [*turns toward* ARGAN; *majestically*] Six, eight, or ten; always according to the even numbers; as medicines are administered according to the odd numbers.

ARGAN [*bows*] Good day, sir.

DIAFOIRUS [*bows; notices* THOMAS *and* TOINETTE. *Sharply*] Thomas!

[*Points to exit.* THOMAS, *in a panic, runs up steps, under his father's outstretched arm.* THOMAS *stops, faces audi-*

ence. DIAFOIRUS *joins him, faces audience. Music. The*
DIAFOIRUSES *about face, exit in cadence. Curtains are*
drawn. Exit TOINETTE. ARGAN *goes to his chair, count-*
ing on his fingers. Enter BÉLINE, *hurriedly.*]

BÉLINE My darling, I had to stop on my way out to tell
you something terrible! I was just going past Angélique's
door, and I saw a *man* with her, a young man! As soon as
he saw me he ran away.

ARGAN A young man with my daughter!

BÉLINE Yes. Your daughter Louison was with them, and
she can tell you something.

ARGAN Send her here, my love, send her here. [*Exit*
BÉLINE. ARGAN *takes a switch from the medicine table, hides*
it behind his back, sits in his chair.] Oh, the brazen creature!
Now I understand why she resisted.

[*Enter* LOUISON, *carrying a doll in her arms. She stops*
in midstage, occupying herself with doll.]

LOUISON What do you want, Papa dear? Stepmother said
you were looking for me.

ARGAN [*with feigned kindliness*] Yes. Come here. [*She*
advances two steps.] Farther. [*She takes two more steps.*]
Turn around. [*She faces him.*] Raise your head. [*She obeys.*]
Look at me. [*She does so. Suddenly and sharply*] Hey?

LOUISON What is it, Papa?

ARGAN Well?

LOUISON What?

ARGAN Haven't you something to tell me?

LOUISON I'll tell you about Red Riding Hood, if you want
to hear a nice story. Or I can recite the poem about the Fox
and the Crow.

ARGAN That's not what I'm asking you.

LOUISON What is it then?

ARGAN Oh, you sly little thing, you know very well what
I mean.

LOUISON Oh no, I beg your pardon, Papa.

ARGAN [*severely*] Is that the way you obey me?

LOUISON What way?

ARGAN Didn't I tell you to come and tell me right away anything you saw?

LOUISON Yes, Papa.

ARGAN And did you do it?

LOUISON Yes, Papa. I came and told you everything I saw.

ARGAN And didn't you see anything today?

LOUISON No, Papa.

ARGAN No?

LOUISON No, Papa.

ARGAN You're sure?

LOUISON Oh yes, I'm sure, Papa.

ARGAN Well now, I'm going to show *you* something.

[*Pulls out the switch.*]

LOUISON Oh, Papa!

ARGAN [*rising, approaching* LOUISON] Aha, you bad little girl, you wouldn't tell me that you saw a man in your sister's room?

LOUISON Papa!

ARGAN [*takes her by the wrist; doll falls to floor. He flourishes switch*] Here's something which will teach you to lie!

LOUISON [*falling on her knees*] Oh Papa, I ask your pardon. You see, sister told me not to tell you, but I'll tell you everything.

ARGAN First you must be whipped for lying. Then afterwards, we'll see.

LOUISON Forgive me, Papa.

ARGAN No, no.

LOUISON Dear Papa, don't whip me.

ARGAN Yes I will.

LOUISON Papa, Papa, please don't whip me.

ARGAN That's enough.

[*He whips her twice.*]

LOUISON Oh, Papa, you hurt me! Oh, you've killed me, I think.

[*She collapses on floor and lies motionless.*]

ARGAN What's this, what's this? Louison! Louison! Oh my God! Louison! [*He kneels behind her, facing audience. Shakes her.*] Heaven help me, she's really dead! Oh misery, what have I done? Curses on the switch! The devil take the switch! [*He throws it away, and crouches over* LOUISON.] Oh, my poor darling, my poor little Louison!

LOUISON [*sits up*] There, there, Papa, don't cry so much; I'm not quite dead.

ARGAN Well! What a sly little creature! [*He rises, picks her up.*] Oh, all right; I'll pardon you this time, on condition that you tell me everything straight.

LOUISON Oh yes, Papa.

ARGAN [*leads her to the bed platform, sits on bed, seats* LOUISON *on his knee.*] Now at least be very careful, for there's my little finger, which knows everything, and it will tell me if you lie.

LOUISON But Papa, don't tell sister I told you.

ARGAN Oh no.

LOUISON Well then, Papa, a man came into sister's room when I was there.

ARGAN Well then?

LOUISON I asked him what he wanted, and he said he was her singing teacher.

ARGAN Oho! So that's it! Well then?

LOUISON She said to him: "Get out, get out! Dear God, get out! You'll drive me mad!"

ARGAN Well then?

LOUISON He didn't want to get out.

ARGAN What did he say to her?

LOUISON He said—oh, a lot of things.

ARGAN And what else?

LOUISON He said all this and all that, he loved her a lot, and she was the prettiest girl in the world.

ARGAN Then what?

LOUISON Then he got down on his knees in front of her.

ARGAN And then what?

LOUISON And then he kissed her hands.

ARGAN [*very apprehensive*] And then what?

LOUISON Then stepmother came to the door, and he ran away.

ARGAN [*much relieved*] There wasn't anything else?

LOUISON No, Papa.

ARGAN Still, there's my little finger mumbling something. Wait a minute. [*Puts little finger in his ear.*] What? Aha! Yes? Oho! There's my little finger telling me you saw something and you haven't told me.

LOUISON Oh Papa, your little finger is a story-teller.

ARGAN Look out!

LOUISON No, Papa, don't believe him; he's telling fibs, I know.

ARGAN Oh all right; we'll see about that. Now run along. And keep your eyes open. [*Puts her down.*] Run away. [LOUISON *picks up doll, curtseys to* ARGAN, *and runs out.*] Oh, there aren't any children any more. [*Rises stiffly, steps down from platform.*] Oh, what a lot of trouble! [*His eye catches the medicine table. He runs to it.*] I don't even have time to think about my illness. [*Pours some medicine into a glass and sips it.*] Really, I can't stand it much longer.

[*Leans on table.*]

[*Enter* BÉRALDE, *side entrance.*]

BÉRALDE How d'ye do, brother Argan? How are you today?

ARGAN Ah, brother, I'm pretty bad.

[*Puts down glass.*]

BÉRALDE What do you mean, pretty bad?

ARGAN [*goes to his chair, leans on it*] Yes, I'm so weak you can hardly believe it.

BÉRALDE [*lightly*] That's too bad.

ARGAN I am hardly able to speak.

BÉRALDE [*discounting* ARGAN's *complaints*] Brother Argan, I've come to propose to you a match for my niece Angélique.

ARGAN [*furious, shouting*] Brother, don't mention that

good-for-nothing to me! She's an impudent, impertinent rap-scallion, and I'll put her in a convent before two days are up.

BÉRALDE Why, all right, all right. I am glad your strength is coming back; my visit is doing you good. [ARGAN *shrugs his shoulders, collapses in chair.*] Now, now, we'll talk of business later. I've brought along some performers; they will cheer you up and put you in a better state of mind for our discussion. They are some gypsies dressed up as Moors; they will dance and sing for you, and I think they'll do you more good than one of Dr. Purgon's prescriptions. All right—

END OF ACT II

SECOND ENTR'ACTE

[*Enter* TOINETTE, *who moves the chairs to the side of the stage. Musical overture. Enter a troupe of gypsies, who sing songs in praise of love, and perform various dances, in one of which their pet monkeys participate. The text of the songs is here omitted.*]

ACT III

[*The rear curtains have been closed during the entr'acte. At its end,* TOINETTE, *supporting* ARGAN, *leads him to his chair in its old position.* BÉRALDE *follows.*]

BÉRALDE Well, brother, what do you say to that? Isn't that as good as a dose of castor oil?

TOINETTE Hmm; good castor oil is good.

[*She establishes* ARGAN *in his chair.*]

BÉRALDE Now look, wouldn't you like to have a little talk?

ARGAN [*seized by pangs*] Be patient a minute, brother, I'll be right back.

[*He rises and moves rapidly toward exit.*]

TOINETTE Wait a minute, sir, you've forgotten that you can't walk without your stick.

[*She hands stick to* ARGAN, *takes him by the shoulders and pushes him toward exit.*]

ARGAN You're right.

[*Exit.*]

TOINETTE [*confidentially, to* BÉRALDE] Please, you're going to help your niece out, aren't you?

BÉRALDE I will do everything I can to obtain for her what she desires.

TOINETTE We must absolutely prevent this fantastic marriage he's got into his head, and I thought it would be a good idea if I could bring in here a doctor of our own, to disgust him with his Dr. Purgon and his way of handling the case. But as we haven't got anybody on hand for that, I'd thought of playing a little trick.

BÉRALDE What do you mean?

TOINETTE Well, it's kind of crazy. But perhaps it will turn out better than if it was sensible. You just let me alone; and you do what you can. Here he is now.

[The two separate and assume an innocent expression. Enter ARGAN *sulkily. "Any luck?" inquires* TOINETTE *in dumbshow. "None at all,"* ARGAN *indicates.* TOINETTE *mimics her grieved sympathy. She takes his cane, hangs it on back of easy chair, helps him to sit. She puts a wash-basin on floor before him, pours water in it from a jug, which she places beside chair. Exit* TOINETTE. ARGAN *removes slippers, places one on each side of basin, removes stockings.]*

BÉRALDE *[after watching* ARGAN *commiseratingly, takes up his subject in a soothing voice]* My dear brother, I should like to ask you especially not to let yourself get excited.

ARGAN That's all right.

          [He throws a stocking back over his shoulder.]

BÉRALDE And not to show any ill humor at anything I may say.

ARGAN Yes.

BÉRALDE And to deal with the matters under discussion with a calm mind, without any emotion.

ARGAN Good God, yes. *[Throws second stocking over his shoulder.* BÉRALDE *fetches a chair for himself.]* My, what an introduction.

          [He dips his toe cautiously in the water. It is too hot; he lifts his foot high.]

BÉRALDE *[places his chair beside* ARGAN's *and sits down]* How does it happen, my dear brother, that with all your money, and with only one daughter, for I'm not counting the little one, how does it happen, I say, that you talk of putting her into a convent?

ARGAN How does it happen, my dear brother, that I am master in my own house to do whatever seems best to me?

BÉRALDE Your wife is always advising you to get rid of your two daughters in this way, and I have no doubt that out of pure charity she would be delighted to see them both holy nuns.

ARGAN Oh, now we're coming to it! *[Incautiously dips his*

foot in the water; he lifts it in pain and anger.] My poor wife is mixed up in it now. She's the one who makes all the trouble, and everybody has it in for her.

BÉRALDE No, no, brother. We'll leave her out of it. She's a woman who has the best intentions in the world for your family; there's nothing selfish about her; she has a remarkable love for you, and she shows your children an affection and kindness which are hardly conceivable; that's certain. Let's not talk of her, but come back to your daughter. What is your idea in marrying her to a doctor's son?

ARGAN [*putting his feet, one after the other, in the water, with the utmost precaution*] My idea, my dear brother, is to get the right sort of son-in-law.

BÉRALDE Yes, but brother, that isn't quite the thing for your daughter, and there's a match proposed which is much more suitable for her.

ARGAN Yes, but brother, this match is more suitable for me.

BÉRALDE But should her future husband be for her or for you?

ARGAN He should be, my dear brother, both for her and for me, and I want to get into my family the people I need.

BÉRALDE According to that reasoning, if your little Louison were grown up, you would give her an apothecary for a husband.

ARGAN [*innocently*] Why not?

BÉRALDE [*disgusted, rises and paces stage*] Is it possible that you will always be so infatuated with your apothecaries and physicians, and that you insist on being sick in spite of everybody and in spite of nature?

ARGAN What do you mean by that, my dear brother?

BÉRALDE [*sharply; irritated*] I mean that I've never seen anyone who is less sick than you are, and I couldn't ask for a better constitution than yours. [ARGAN *shrugs his shoulders.* BÉRALDE *masters his anger, comes to* ARGAN's *side. Bantering*] A very good sign that you are well, and that you have a strong and vigorous body, is that with all the medical care you've had, you haven't yet succeeded in ruining your system, and you haven't died of all the medicines they've made you take.

ARGAN [*tragically*] But don't you know that that's what keeps me going, and that Dr. Purgon says I would pass away if he shouldn't be able to take care of me for even three days?

BÉRALDE If you don't look out, he will take such good care of you that he will send you to the other world.

ARGAN [*has finally got both feet solidly in the water. He sits back. BÉRALDE sits. As discussion proceeds, ARGAN becomes more and more excited, shouts louder and louder.*] But just let's talk this over for a moment. So you don't believe in medicine?

BÉRALDE No, brother, and for health's sake I don't see that it is necessary to believe in it.

ARGAN What! you don't accept as true a thing which has been agreed upon by everybody, and which has been revered by all past time?

BÉRALDE Far from accepting it as true, I find it, between you and me, one of the greatest follies of mankind; and if I look at it from a philosophical point of view, I've never seen a sillier lot of humbuggery. I don't think there is anything more ridiculous than that one man should undertake to cure another.

ARGAN And why, pray, shouldn't one man be able to cure another?

BÉRALDE For this reason: that the functioning of man's machine has been a mystery, up to the present, and man has hardly been able to understand anything of it. Nature has put before our eyes some veils too thick for us to be able to penetrate them.

ARGAN So doctors don't know anything, according to you?

BÉRALDE Oh yes they do. Most of them have had a very good education, they know how to talk very good Latin, and how to name all the diseases in Greek, and define them and classify them; but as for curing them, that's what they don't know at all.

ARGAN But you must still admit that on this subject the doctors know more than other people.

BÉRALDE My dear brother, they know just what I have told you, which isn't very much. All the excellence of their art consists in a pompous jargon, in a fine high-sounding lingo, which gives you words for reasons and promises for results.

ARGAN But after all, there are people as sensible as you are; and we see that in time of sickness everybody calls in the doctors.

BÉRALDE That's an indication of human weakness, not of the genuineness of their art.

ARGAN But the doctors must certainly think their art is genuine, since they use it on themselves.

BÉRALDE The fact is that there are some among them who accept the popular delusion, by which they profit, and others who profit by it without accepting the delusion. Your Dr. Purgon, for instance, doesn't know any better; he is a man who is all doctor, from head to foot, a man who believes in his rules more than in all the demonstrations of mathematics, who would think it a crime to venture to examine his rules. He doesn't see anything obscure in medicine, or anything doubtful or difficult. With his impetuous prejudice, his rigid self-confidence, his brutality in applying what he thinks is reasonable, he gives his purgings and his bleedings, come what come may, and he never pauses to consider anything. You shouldn't hold any grudge against him for anything he may do to you; it's with the best faith in the world that he will finish you off, and in killing you he will do just what he has done to his wife and children, and what, if the occasion should arise, he will do to himself.

ARGAN The fact is, brother, you just never have liked him. [*Pours more hot water from jug into basin. Resigned gesture by* BÉRALDE.] But anyway, let's come to the point. What should you do when you're sick?

BÉRALDE Nothing, my dear brother.

ARGAN [*amazed*] Nothing?

BÉRALDE Nothing. Just stay quiet. When we let nature alone, she recovers by herself from the disorder she's fallen into. It's our disquiet, our impatience which upsets everything; and most men die of their remedies, and not of their illnesses.

ARGAN But you must agree that we can aid that nature in certain ways.

BÉRALDE [*becoming excited*] Dear heaven, those are mere ideas that we like to befool ourselves with. Men have always been full of fine fancies which we come to believe because they flatter us, and because it would be very nice if they were true. When a doctor talks to you about aiding, supporting, relieving nature, about taking from nature what interferes with her and supplying her what she lacks, about restoring nature and making her function properly; when he talks to you about rectifying the blood, tempering the vital organs and the brain, readjusting the lungs, repairing the liver and fortifying the heart, about his having secrets to make you live years longer, he is telling you medicine's fairy tale. But when you come down to truth and experience, you find nothing of all that; it's like one of those lovely dreams which leave you, when you wake up, only the distress of having believed them.

ARGAN [*angrily*] That is to say that all the knowledge in the world is shut up in your head, and you think you know more than all the great medical men of our time.

BÉRALDE In speech and action, your great medical men are two different sorts of people. To hear them talk, they're the most skillful people on earth; but in action, they're the most ignorant men alive.

ARGAN Yeah! You're a great doctor, I can see that. I wish that one of those gentlemen were here to answer your arguments and make you sing small for a change.

BÉRALDE [*yielding, out of policy*] Why, brother, I don't take it on myself to fight medicine. Everybody, at his own risk and peril, can believe what he likes. What I am saying is just between us two. I would have liked to save you from some of your mistakes; and to cheer you up, I would have liked to take you to see a comedy of Molière.

ARGAN [*annoyed*] He's an impudent fellow, that Molière of yours; and that's a fine business, for him to make fun of honest men like doctors.

BÉRALDE It isn't the doctors he makes fun of, but the absurdities of doctoring.

ARGAN And what business is it of his to criticize doctoring? He's a stupid, impertinent fool, to make fun of consultations and prescriptions, to attack the honorable corps of physicians, and to go and put on his stage distinguished people like those gentlemen.

BÉRALDE What should he put on his stage, if not the various professions of men? Every day you can see princes and kings on the stage, and they certainly stand as high as doctors do.

ARGAN Oh, the devil! If I were the doctors, I'd get back at him for his insolence; and when he gets sick, I'd let him die without giving him any help. Let him say and do what he likes, I wouldn't prescribe the slightest little bleeding, the smallest little enema; and I'd say to him: "Croak! Croak! That will teach you next time to make fun of the Faculty of Medicine!"

BÉRALDE He certainly makes you angry.

ARGAN Yes, he's a trouble-making fool, and if the doctors have any sense, they will do what I say.

BÉRALDE He will have more sense than your doctors, for he won't ask them for any help.

ARGAN All the worse for him, if he won't seek the benefit of their remedies.

BÉRALDE He has his reasons not to want any, and he maintains that that is only permissible for vigorous, robust people who have strength and to spare to bear the remedies with the disease; but as for him, he has only strength enough to bear his illness.

ARGAN What a lot of rubbish! Look, let's not talk about that man any more; that rouses my bile, and you'd be likely to give me his sickness.

[*Pours more hot water in his basin and settles back.*]

BÉRALDE All right, brother; and to change the subject I will tell you that just because your daughter objects to your plans you shouldn't make so violent a decision as to put her in a convent. And I'll say that in choosing a son-in-law, you shouldn't follow blindly this passion which possesses you, and that in these circumstances you should accommodate yourself a little to your daughter's inclinations, since it's for all her life, and all the happiness of a marriage is at stake.

[*Music. Rear curtains open, revealing* MONSIEUR FLEURANT, *a fussy, dapper, choleric apothecary, bearing an enormous syringe. To music, he comes downstage, steps on bed platform, beckons to* ARGAN *to approach, and prepares to give enema.*]

ARGAN [*putting on slippers*] Oh brother, if you will permit me—

BÉRALDE How's that? What do you want to do?

ARGAN To take this little enema. It will be just a moment.

[*He rises.*]

BÉRALDE Don't be foolish. [*Thrusts* ARGAN *back in his chair.*] Can't you be a moment without an enema or a purge? Put it off till some other time, and stay quiet a while.

ARGAN [*overawed*] Monsieur Fleurant, we'll leave it till this evening or tomorrow morning.

FLEURANT [*advances on* BÉRALDE *threateningly*] What business is it of yours to oppose the prescriptions of medicine and to prevent this gentleman from taking my enema? I'm amazed at your effrontery.

BÉRALDE [*advances toward* FLEURANT] Come, sir, come; it's clear that you aren't used to talking to people's faces.

FLEURANT [*screaming with rage*] You have no right to make light of medicine and make me lose my time. [BÉRALDE *takes him by the arm and pushes him backward.*] I came here by doctor's orders with a proper prescription, and I'll tell Dr. Purgon [BÉRALDE *again thrusts him backward*] how I have been prevented from executing his orders and doing my duty. [*Goes to rear, up two steps, and turns back to* BÉRALDE.] You will see! [*Moves toward exit, turns back again.*] You will see!

[*Exit. Rear curtains are drawn.*]

ARGAN Brother, I'm afraid you're going to be the cause of some dreadful misfortune.

BÉRALDE [*returning downstage*] What a misfortune it is, not to take an enema Dr. Purgon has ordered! Once more, brother, is it possible there is no way to cure you of the disease of doctors? Do you want to spend your whole life tortured by their remedies?

ARGAN Good heavens, you talk about it like a well man; but if you were in my place, you would change your tune quick enough. It's easy to talk against medicine when you're in good health.

BÉRALDE But just what is your illness anyway?

ARGAN You'll drive me crazy! I wish that you had my illness; we'd see if you'd talk so much.

[*Roll of drums. Rear curtains open, revealing* DR. PURGON, *standing majestically, forefinger upraised.* FLEURANT *is beside him, happily foreseeing* ARGAN's *punishment. Enter* TOINETTE *from side.*]

ARGAN Aha! Here's Dr. Purgon!

[PURGON *advances impressively, to music.* FLEURANT *remains on rear platform.* ARGAN *is terrified.*]

PURGON [*slowly, ominously*] I have just heard, here at your door, a pretty piece of news, that my prescriptions are being trifled with, that there has been a refusal to take the remedy which I had prescribed.

ARGAN Doctor, it isn't . . .

PURGON That is very great audacity, and a very strange rebellion of a patient against his physician.

TOINETTE How appalling!

PURGON [*turning toward* TOINETTE] An enema which I had taken pleasure in composing myself.

ARGAN It wasn't me!

PURGON [*turning toward* ARGAN] Invented and drawn up according to all the rules of the art.

TOINETTE He was quite wrong.

PURGON [*turning toward* TOINETTE] And which was destined to have in the intestinal tract a most marvellous effect.

ARGAN It was my brother . . .

PURGON [*facing audience*] To reject it with scorn!

ARGAN He was the one . . .

PURGON [*taking step toward* ARGAN] It was an unimaginable action.

TOINETTE That's right.

PURGON [*taking another step toward* ARGAN] A monstrous crime against Medicine.

ARGAN He was responsible . . .

PURGON [*another step toward* ARGAN] A crime of contempt of Faculty which cannot be sufficiently punished.

TOINETTE Absolutely right.

PURGON [*beside* ARGAN's *chair. He draws himself up imposingly*] I declare to you that I break off all relations with you.

ARGAN It was my brother . . .

PURGON That I no longer wish to have any family alliance with you.

TOINETTE Quite right too.

PURGON And in order to put an end to all our dealings, here is the settlement I was making on my nephew in favor of his marriage.

[*He tears up the settlement, throws pieces on floor, stamps on them. He proceeds upstage.*]

ARGAN It was my brother who made all the trouble.

PURGON [*at foot of steps, turns sharply on* ARGAN] To scorn my enema!

ARGAN Bring it here, I'll take it right away!

[*He rises from his chair, runs to bed, climbs on it,
crouches on it, his back to audience.*]

PURGON [*advancing step by step toward bed*] I would
have cured you in no time at all.

TOINETTE He doesn't deserve it.

PURGON I was going to cleanse your whole body and
evacuate entirely the evil humors.

ARGAN [*collapses on bed in sitting position*] Oh, my
brother!

PURGON And I only needed a dozen medications to clean
up the whole business.

TOINETTE He is unworthy to be treated by you.

PURGON [*jumps on bed platform.* ARGAN, *in terror, leans
backward, supporting himself on his elbows.* PURGON *bends
over him savagely.*] But since you wouldn't be cured through
my ministrations . . .

ARGAN It isn't my fault.

PURGON Since you have departed from the obedience
which one owes to one's physician . . .

TOINETTE He's got to pay for it.

PURGON Since you have declared yourself a rebel against
the remedies which I prescribed for you . . .

ARGAN Oh, not at all.

PURGON I have only to tell you that I abandon you to
your bad constitution, to the disorder of your intestinal
tract, to the corruption of your blood, to the bitterness of
your bile, and to the turbidity of your humors.

[*He moves rapidly to the rear, and begins to mount
steps.*]

TOINETTE And a very good thing too.

ARGAN [*falls flat on bed, his face in his hands*] My God!

PURGON [*turns on step, raises right forefinger, thunders
at* ARGAN] And I hope that within four days you will fall
into an incurable state.

ARGAN [*falls out of bed, scrambles to foot of steps, holds
up clasped hands to* PURGON] Mercy!

PURGON And that you may fall into the clutch of gastritis . . .

> [*Points his forefinger at* ARGAN.]

ARGAN [*falls on his knees*] Dr. Purgon!

PURGON [*raising forefinger*] And from gastritis into colitis . . .

> [*Points forefinger. The same business is repeated during following speeches.*]

ARGAN Dr. Purgon!

PURGON And from colitis into enteritis . . .

ARGAN Dr. Purgon!

PURGON And from enteritis into hepatitis . . .

ARGAN Dr. Purgon!

PURGON And from hepatitis into appendicitis . . .

ARGAN Dr. Purgon!

PURGON And from appendicitis into peritonitis . . .

ARGAN Dr. Purgon!

PURGON And from peritonitis to the extinction of life, which will be the final result of your folly.

> [*Turns and goes rapidly out rear exit.* FLEURANT *laughs diabolically. Curtains are drawn.* TOINETTE *exits at side, laughing.* ARGAN *lies flat on floor.*]

ARGAN Dear God, I'm a dead man. Brother, you have killed me.

BÉRALDE What? What's the matter?

ARGAN I'm done for. I can feel already that Medicine is taking its revenge on me.

BÉRALDE Dear brother, you're crazy. [*Picks up* ARGAN *from floor, helps him impatiently to his chair, settles him in it.*] For a good deal I wouldn't like people to see you acting this way. Just examine yourself a little. Get hold of yourself, and don't give in so much to your imagination.

ARGAN [*groaning, with chattering teeth*] You heard the terrible diseases he threatened me with.

BÉRALDE Really, how simple you are.

ARGAN He said I would become incurable in less than four days.

BÉRALDE Yes, but what he says has nothing to do with the facts. Was that an oracle that spoke? To hear you, it would seem that Dr. Purgon holds the thread of your life in his hands, and by some mighty authority he extends it and shortens it as he pleases. Just reflect that the principles of your life are within yourself, and that Dr. Purgon's anger can't make you die any more than his remedies can make you live. [*Pause.* BÉRALDE *recalls* TOINETTE'S *proposal, at beginning of act.*] This episode ought to bring you to the point of getting free of all doctors; or if you're born to be a man who can't do without them, it's easy to get another, with whom you may run a little less risk.

ARGAN Oh brother, he knows my whole constitution and the way I should take care of it.

BÉRALDE I must say you're a man of fixed ideas; you certainly see things from a strange point of view.

[*Enter* TOINETTE, *busy and bustling. She picks up* ARGAN'S *basin, puts it under medicine table.*]

TOINETTE Monsieur, there's a doctor here who wants to see you.

ARGAN What doctor?

TOINETTE [*puts jug beside basin*] A medical doctor.

ARGAN I'm asking you who he is.

TOINETTE [*between* ARGAN *and* BÉRALDE] I don't know him; but he looks a lot like me [*she winks at* BÉRALDE], and if I weren't sure that my mother was an honest woman, I would say he is probably some little brother she's given me after my father's death.

ARGAN Bring him in. [*Exit* TOINETTE, *quickly.*]

BÉRALDE That's a bit of good luck. One doctor leaves you, and another shows up.

ARGAN I am very much afraid that you will be the cause of some terrible misfortune.

BÉRALDE What, again? You keep coming back to that.

ARGAN You see, I'm oppressed by all those diseases I don't know about, those . . .

[*Music. Rear curtains open.* TOINETTE, *in doctor's gown,*

*wig, and toque, is revealed. Large spectacles. She comes
downstage, to music. She imitates the manner of* DR.
DIAFOIRUS.]

TOINETTE Monsieur, permit me to pay you my respects
and to offer to you my best services for all the bleedings and
purges you may need.

[*Bows deeply.*]

ARGAN [*bowing*] Sir, I am deeply obliged to you. [*To*
BÉRALDE] My faith, he looks just like Toinette.

TOINETTE Sir, I beg you to excuse me a moment. I forgot to give an order to my servant. I will be right back.

[*Exits, rear, with a combination of haste and dignity.*]

ARGAN Eh, wouldn't you say it really is Toinette?

BÉRALDE It's true there is a very great resemblance; but it
isn't the first time that has happened. There are innumerable
cases of these tricks of nature.

ARGAN As for me, I am much surprised, and . . .

[*Enter* TOINETTE, *side, in her ordinary costume. She is
very matter-of-fact.*]

TOINETTE What did you want, sir?

ARGAN What?

TOINETTE Didn't you call me?

ARGAN Me? No.

TOINETTE My ears must have been burning.

[*She starts to go.*]

ARGAN Wait here a minute and see how much the doctor
looks like you.

TOINETTE Yes, indeed! I'm busy downstairs. I've seen him
plenty already.

[*Exit, side.*]

ARGAN [*watches her go*] If I hadn't seen them both, I
would have thought it was the same person.

BÉRALDE I have read some very surprising examples of
such resemblances as this; there have been some cases in our
own times which have fooled everybody.

ARGAN As for me, I would have been fooled by this case;
I would have sworn it's the same person.

[*Enter* TOINETTE, *in doctor's costume, rear. She is un-hurried.*]

TOINETTE Sir, I most earnestly beg your pardon.

[*Bows.*]

ARGAN [*to* BÉRALDE] It is really extraordinary.

TOINETTE I trust that you will not take amiss the curiosity I have felt to see so distinguished an invalid as you are; and your reputation, which has extended far, may excuse the liberty I have taken.

ARGAN Sir, I am at your service.

TOINETTE I see, sir, that you are looking at me very attentively. How old do you think I am?

ARGAN I think that at the most you may be twenty-six or twenty-seven.

TOINETTE Ha, ha, ha! I am ninety.

ARGAN Ninety?

TOINETTE Yes. You see the results of the secrets of my art, which keep me thus fresh and vigorous.

[*She executes a pirouette.*]

ARGAN My word, there's a fine young old gentleman for ninety.

TOINETTE I am a roving doctor. I go from city to city, from province to province, from country to country, in order to study matters worthy of my attention and invalids worthy of my interest, who may be fit subjects for the great secrets I have discovered in medical science. I scorn to waste my time on all the trifling everyday illnesses, trivial rheumatisms and catarrhs, wretched little fevers, vapors and migraines. What I want is important diseases, good long fevers with delirium, fine high fevers with purple eruptions, good old plagues, nice well-formed dropsies, splendid pleurisies with inflammation of the lungs. That's what I like, that's where I triumph. [*Bends over* ARGAN, *pointing her finger at him.*] And I should be delighted, sir, if you had all the diseases I have just named, and if you were given up by all the doctors, in desperation, in your last agony [*straightens up, smiling, and bows*] just so I could show you the excellence of my cures, and my earnest desire to render you service.

ARGAN [*disconsolately*] I am much obliged to you, sir, for all your kindness to me.

TOINETTE Give me your pulse. [*He extends his arm apprehensively. A pause; she shakes his arm.*] Come on, beat properly. Oh, I'll make you behave. [*Shakes his arm violently.*] Oho! This pulse is trying to cut up; I see it doesn't know me yet. [*Flings* ARGAN's *arm from her; it hits the chair-arm; he grimaces. In a scornful tone*] Who is your doctor?

ARGAN Dr. Purgon.

TOINETTE Purgon? That name is not on my list of the great doctors. What does he say is your illness?

ARGAN He says it's the liver. [TOINETTE *indicates amazement.*] But others say it's the spleen.

TOINETTE [*rolls up her sleeves, taps* ARGAN's *chest smartly; goes behind his chair, bends his head back, inspects his eyes, opens his mouth.* ARGAN *sticks out his tongue; she feels it with her finger. She closes his mouth by clapping him under the chin;* ARGAN *bites his tongue. She returns to face him.*] They are all blockheads. It's the lungs that are causing the trouble.

ARGAN The lungs?

TOINETTE [*facing audience, with air of knowing all the answers, and seeking only supporting evidence*] Yes. How do you feel?

ARGAN Sometimes I feel pains in my head.

TOINETTE Exactly. The lungs.

ARGAN It seems to me sometimes I have a cloud in front of my eyes.

TOINETTE The lungs.

ARGAN Sometimes I have pains in my heart.

TOINETTE The lungs.

ARGAN And occasionally I feel a general weakness in all my limbs.

TOINETTE Lungs.

ARGAN And sometimes I have pains in my stomach, as if it were colic.

TOINETTE Lungs. Do you have much appetite for what you eat?

ARGAN [*smiling*] Yes, Doctor.

TOINETTE [*pokes him suddenly in the breast*] Lungs. [ARGAN *shrinks back.*] You like to drink a little wine?

ARGAN Yes, Doctor.

TOINETTE Lungs. You feel sleepy after your meals, and you're glad to take a little nap?

ARGAN Yes, Doctor.

TOINETTE Lungs, lungs, I tell you. What does your doctor order for your diet?

ARGAN He orders soup.

TOINETTE Blockhead!

ARGAN And fowl.

TOINETTE Blockhead!

ARGAN Veal.

TOINETTE Blockhead!

ARGAN Bouillons.

TOINETTE Blockhead!

ARGAN Fresh eggs.

TOINETTE [*horrified*] Blockhead!

ARGAN And in the evening, prunes to relax the bowels.

TOINETTE [*with a scornful laugh*] Blockhead!

ARGAN And especially, to take my wine with a lot of water.

TOINETTE Ignorantus, ignoranta, ignorantum! You must drink your wine straight, and to thicken your blood, which is too dilute, you must eat good rich beef, good rich pork, good Holland cheese, grits and rice, chestnuts and cakes, in order to solidify and conglutinate the system. Your doctor is a fool. I am going to send you a competent one, and I will come and see you from time to time, as long as I am in the city.

ARGAN [*with a gesture of gratitude with his left arm*] You will oblige me very much.

TOINETTE [*grabbing his arm*] What the devil are you doing with that arm?

ARGAN [*terrified*] What?

TOINETTE There's an arm I would have cut off immediately, if I were you.

ARGAN Why?

TOINETTE Don't you realize that it draws all the nourishment to itself, and it prevents that whole side from profiting by it?

ARGAN [*pulls back his arm, protects it with his right arm*] Yes, but I need my arm.

TOINETTE [*points at his right eye.* ARGAN *protects it with his hand*] You've got a right eye there that I would get rid of, if I were in your place.

ARGAN Get rid of an eye?

TOINETTE Don't you see that it incapacitates the other eye and deprives it of its proper nourishment? Believe me, you should get rid of it as soon as possible, and you will see much better with the left eye.

ARGAN There's no hurry.

TOINETTE [*with gesture of resignation*] Well, good-bye. I am sorry to leave you so soon, but I have to be at an important conference at the bedside of a man who died yesterday.

[*Moves toward rear.*]

ARGAN [*bewildered*] A man who died yesterday?

TOINETTE [*on rear steps*] Yes, to consult about what ought to have been done to cure him. Good-bye.

[*Bows deeply.*]

ARGAN You know that patients cannot see you to the door.
[TOINETTE *bows again, exits with dignity. The curtains are drawn.*]

BÉRALDE [*suppressing a desire to laugh*] There is a doctor who seems to know his business.

ARGAN Yes, but he goes a little too quick.

BÉRALDE All great physicians are like that.

ARGAN Cut off my arm, put out my eye, so that the others

will do better! I'd a good deal rather they didn't do so well.
That's a fine operation, to make me one-eyed and one-armed!

[*Enter* TOINETTE, *from side.*]

TOINETTE [*speaking into wings*] All right, all right, excuse me, please. I'm in no mood for fun.

ARGAN What's all this?

TOINETTE Why, it's your doctor, who wanted to feel my
pulse.

[*She goes to the bed and rearranges bedclothes.*]

ARGAN Well, think of that, at the age of ninety.

BÉRALDE Look here, since you've broken off with Dr.
Purgon, don't you want me to say something about the offer
that has been made for your daughter's hand?

ARGAN [*ill-humored again*] No, brother; I want to put her
in a convent, since she has opposed my wishes. I can see
very well there's some love-affair at the bottom of all this,
and I've discovered a certain secret interview that they don't
know I've discovered.

BÉRALDE Well, even if there were some small inclination,
would that be so criminal, and can a trifle offend you, when
it all leads to an honorable end like marriage?

ARGAN However that may be, brother, she will be a nun;
that's settled.

BÉRALDE You want to do pleasure to someone.

ARGAN I understand you. You always come back to that;
you have my poor wife on the brain.

BÉRALDE [*getting angry*] Well, yes, since I must speak
frankly, it's your wife I mean; and just as I can't bear your
obsession with medicine, I can't bear your obsession with her;
and I hate to see you running headlong into all the traps
she lays for you.

TOINETTE [*descends from platform, joins the pair*] Oh,
sir, don't speak of Madame; she's a woman you can't say anything against, all frank and above-board, and how she loves
Monsieur Argan, oh, how she loves him! There aren't any
words for it.

ARGAN [*to* BÉRALDE] Just ask her how she coddles me.

TOINETTE That's right.

ARGAN And how worried she is about my illness.

TOINETTE Absolutely.

ARGAN And all the trouble and care she takes for me.

TOINETTE That's certain. [*To* BÉRALDE] Do you want me to convince you and show you in a minute how Madame loves Monsieur? [*To* ARGAN] Monsieur, let me show him how simple he is, and prove he's mistaken.

ARGAN How do you mean?

TOINETTE Madame is just coming in. You stretch out there [*indicates bed*] and pretend to be dead. You will see how she grieves when I tell her the news.

ARGAN [*reflects a moment*] I'm willing.

[*Rises, goes toward bed.*]

TOINETTE [*accompanying* ARGAN] Yes, but don't leave her in despair very long, for she might die of it.

ARGAN Leave it to me.

[*Lies down on bed.*]

TOINETTE [*returns to* BÉRALDE, *hides him behind curtain at side*] Now you hide yourself in this corner.

ARGAN [*sitting up suddenly*] Isn't there some danger in pretending to be dead?

TOINETTE [*returning to* ARGAN, *making him lie down*] No, no. What danger could there be? Just lie down. [*Confidentially*] It will be a pleasure to show up your brother. [*Glances at door.*] Here is Madame now. You stay still. [*Sits on bed platform, her back to bed.*] Oh, dear God! Oh, dear, oh, dear! Oh, what a frightful accident!

BÉLINE [*entering at side*] What's the matter, Toinette?

TOINETTE Oh, Madame!

BÉLINE What is it?

TOINETTE Your husband is dead!

BÉLINE My husband is dead?

TOINETTE Oh, dear, yes. The dear departed has deceased.

BÉLINE You're quite sure?

TOINETTE Quite sure. No one knows anything about it

yet; I was here all by myself. He just passed away in my arms. Look, there he is all stretched out on his bed.

BÉLINE [hesitates a moment, goes to bedside, leans over ARGAN. She straightens up.] Well, heaven be praised! I've got rid of a terrible burden. [TOINETTE sobs. BÉLINE takes some steps toward her.] You're a fool, Toinette, to distress yourself about his death.

TOINETTE Madame, I thought I ought to cry.

BÉLINE Come, come; it isn't worth the trouble. It isn't much of a loss; what good was he on earth? [Moves back toward head of bed, relieving her long pent-up rancor.] A man who was always troublesome to everyone, dirty, disgusting, always with an enema or a purge in him, always blowing his nose, coughing, spitting; stupid, tiresome, sulky, wearing everybody out, scolding the servants all day and all night.

TOINETTE There's a fine funeral oration.

BÉLINE [descends from bed platform, leads TOINETTE to center] Toinette, you must help me to carry out my plan, and you may be sure that you'll get a good reward for helping me. Fortunately no one has been informed yet, so let's say nothing until I have done my little job. There are some papers and some money I'd like to get hold of, and it isn't right that I should have spent the best years of my life with him without some return. [Starts toward door.] Come on, Toinette. [She has a new idea.] But first let's take his keys. [Goes on tiptoe to foot of bed, kneels down to pull out the strong-box under the bed. She opens the box and looks for keys. Meanwhile ARGAN sits up cautiously, moves on all fours to foot of bed, so that his face is above BÉLINE.]

ARGAN [gently] Take it easy.

BÉLINE [springs to her feet and recoils to center of stage] Oh!

ARGAN [stands up on bed] Yes, my dear wife! So that's how you love me!

TOINETTE [collapses, laughing, in ARGAN's easy chair] Ha, ha, ha! The deceased isn't dead!

ARGAN [to BÉLINE] I am very happy to observe your love

for me, and to hear the fine tribute you made to me. [BÉLINE, *who has been staring entranced at* ARGAN, *turns and runs out, with a scream which continues after she is in the wings.*] There is a word to the wise which will come in handy in the future, and which will keep me from doing a lot of things.

BÉRALDE [*has emerged from his hiding-place when* BÉLINE *screamed*] Well, brother, you see.

TOINETTE [*glances offstage*] My word, I never would have believed it. [*Rises; goes to* ARGAN.] But I hear your daughter outside; get back the way you were, and we'll see how she will take the news of your death. [*Tries to persuade* ARGAN *to lie down; he resists.*] Well, there's no harm in trying it out; and now that you've got started, you can learn this way the feelings that your whole family has for you.

[ARGAN *sees* ANGÉLIQUE *offstage, throws himself down and lies motionless.* TOINETTE *hides* BÉRALDE *again, returns to bed-platform, turns her back to* ANGÉLIQUE *and sobs quietly.*]

TOINETTE Oh, heaven! Oh, how terrible! Oh, unlucky day!

ANGÉLIQUE [*enters, stops a moment in surprise, advances to center*] What's the matter, Toinette? Why are you crying?

TOINETTE [*going toward* ANGÉLIQUE] Oh dear, I've some sad news to give you.

ANGÉLIQUE What is it?

TOINETTE Your father is dead.

ANGÉLIQUE My father is dead, Toinette?

TOINETTE Yes; you see him there. He died just a moment ago in a sudden spell of weakness.

ANGÉLIQUE [*remains motionless a moment, starts toward bed. But her courage fails her; she turns and falls, weeping, into* TOINETTE'S *arms*] Oh, dear heaven! What a misfortune! What a cruel blow this is! Oh dear, must I lose my father, all that's left to me in the world, and what's even more dreadful, must I lose him at a time when he was angry with me? What will happen to me now in my trouble, and what consolation can I ever find for losing my father?

[*Enter* CLÉANTE, *cheerily and impetuously. On seeing* ANGÉLIQUE *in tears, he stops, then moves slowly toward* ANGÉLIQUE *and* TOINETTE.]

CLÉANTE What is the matter, my lovely Angélique? What are you crying for?

ANGÉLIQUE Oh dear! I'm crying because I've lost the dearest and most precious thing in my life. I am crying for the death of my father.

CLÉANTE Good heavens, how dreadful! And how sudden! And to think—I had just asked your uncle to make a proposal for me, and I was on my way to see your father and try to move him to accept my offer.

ANGÉLIQUE Oh, Cléante, let's say no more about all that. Let's drop all our thoughts of marriage. After losing my father, I never want to lead a family life; I give it up forever. [*Steps on bed platform.*] Yes, Father, if I have resisted your desires in the past, I now want to follow at least one of your intentions, and make amends for all the grief I know I have given you. [*Kneels.*] Father, permit me to give you my word that I will enter a convent, and let me kiss you to prove my gratitude for all you have done for me. [*Takes* ARGAN'S *hand to kiss it.*]

ARGAN [*sitting up, much moved*] Ah, my dear daughter!

ANGÉLIQUE [*springs from bedside into* TOINETTE'S *arms*] Oh!

[TOINETTE *laughs.* BÉRALDE *emerges from hiding-place.* ARGAN *rises, steps off foot of bed to platform.*]

ARGAN Come my dear, don't be afraid. I'm not dead. [ANGÉLIQUE *flings herself into her father's arms. He embraces her warmly.*] Come, come; you're my own true daughter, and I am delighted to see your real nature.

ANGÉLIQUE Oh, what a wonderful surprise, Father! And now that heaven has given you back to us, to our great joy, let me kneel before you to beg just one thing of you. [*Kneels;* ARGAN *turns his head away.*] If you don't agree to the choice of my own heart, if you refuse to grant me Cléante for a

husband, I beg you at least not to force me to marry anyone
else. And that is the only indulgence I ask of you.

CLÉANTE [*kneels on other side of* ARGAN, *who looks aloft*]
Oh, sir, let yourself be moved by her prayers and by mine,
and do not oppose the honorable love we share.

BÉRALDE [*stepping forward*] Brother, can you hold out
against them?

TOINETTE [*kneeling*] Sir, can you be insensible to so
much love?

ARGAN [*to* BÉRALDE] Let him become a doctor, and I'll
consent to the marriage. [*To* CLÉANTE] Yes, become a doctor,
and I give you my daughter.

CLÉANTE [*springs to his feet.* TOINETTE *rises*] I'll be very
glad to. If that's all I need to be your son-in-law, I'll become
a doctor, and an apothecary too, if you like. [*Raises* ANGÉ-
LIQUE *to her feet and walks with her to side of stage.*] That's
no trouble, and I would do a great deal more to obtain my
beautiful Angélique.

BÉRALDE But brother, I have an idea. Become a doctor
yourself. It would be much more convenient to have everything you need in your own person.

TOINETTE [*to* BÉRALDE] That's right. That's the real way
to get well quick; there's no disease that's so bold as to
trifle with the person of a doctor.

ARGAN Brother, I think you're making fun of me. Am I
of an age to start in studying?

BÉRALDE Studying? Nonsense. You know enough already.
There are plenty of them who don't know as much as you
do.

ARGAN But you have to know how to talk Latin, and
know all the diseases and the remedies for them.

BÉRALDE When you receive the cap and gown of the
doctor, you will learn all that, and afterwards you will know
more than you want to.

ARGAN What! You know how to talk about diseases when
you have that costume on?

BÉRALDE Certainly. You just have to talk. When you have a cap and gown on, any gibberish becomes wisdom, and all nonsense becomes sound reason.

TOINETTE Look sir, if it were only for your beard, that's a lot already; the beard makes more than half the doctor.

CLÉANTE In any case, I'm ready for anything.

BÉRALDE Would you like to have the matter arranged immediately?

ARGAN What do you mean, immediately?

BÉRALDE Yes, right here in your house.

ARGAN In my house?

BÉRALDE Yes. I have some friends on the Faculty who will come immediately to perform the ceremony in your room. It won't cost you anything.

ARGAN But as for me, what do I say? What do I answer?

BÉRALDE They will tell you in just a few words, and they'll give you in writing what you have to read. Now you go and get decently dressed, and I'll send for them.

ARGAN All right, come on, let's do it.

[He descends from bed platform and exits, with TOINETTE accompanying him to exit.]

CLÉANTE [comes downstage with ANGÉLIQUE] But what are you up to, and what do you mean by these friends on the Faculty?

TOINETTE [returning to ANGÉLIQUE's side] What's going on anyway?

BÉRALDE We're going to have a little fun. There's a troupe of actors who have made a skit on the conferring of a doctor's degree, with music and dances. I want to have them put on their act for us, with my brother taking the part of the principal character.

ANGÉLIQUE But Uncle, it seems to me that you're treating my father rather too lightly.

BÉRALDE Well, my dear niece, we aren't so much treating him lightly as accommodating ourselves to his fancies. All this is just in the family. We can each of us take part, and thus put on a show for our own amusement. That's all right in carnival time. So come and get things ready.

CLÉANTE [*to* ANGÉLIQUE] Do you agree?

ANGÉLIQUE Well, all right, since Uncle is taking the responsibility.

[CLÉANTE *and* BÉRALDE *place the arm chair on the bed platform;* TOINETTE *arranges the stools, pushes back the medicine table. Exeunt all.*]

END OF ACT III

FINALE

[NOTE: *This finale is a burlesque, with music and ballet, of the solemn ceremony of the examination and reception of a Doctor of Medicine by the Faculty of the University. As the examinations were conducted in Latin, Molière's text is written in very bad Latin, with intrusions of French and Italian. He could assume that his audience had a sufficient smattering of Latin to enjoy his burlesque. The translator has kept Molière's Latin, but has freely substituted Englishisms for Molière's lapses into French or Italian. Anyone with the slightest tincture of Latin can get the idea, by reading the text fast, without pausing for analysis.*]

[*Music. Rear curtains open. Enter eight syringe-bearers, six apothecaries, with mortars and pestles, twenty-two doctors. Then* ARGAN *with a large roll of paper. Then eight dancing surgeons, two singing surgeons. Then* BÉRALDE *with* LOUISON, ANGÉLIQUE *with* CLÉANTE, TOINETTE. *The presiding officer mounts a portable pulpit. All take their places in a semi-circle around* ARGAN.]

PRESIDING OFFICER   Savantissimi doctores
                             Medicinae professores,
                             Qui hic assemblati estis,
                             Et vos, altri Messiores,
                             Sententiarum Facultatis
                             Fideles executores,
                       Chirurgiani et apothecari,
                     Atque tota compania also,
                             Salus, honor et argentum
                             Atque bonum appetitum.
         [*Orchestra plays a ritornelle, or interlude.*]

                             Non possum, docti confreri,
                             Myselfus satis admirari
                             Qualis bona inventio
                             Est medici professio,

Quam bella thinga est, et bene trovata,
Medicina illa benedicta,
   Quae suo nomine solo,
   Surprisingo miraculo,
   Since so longo tempore
   Facit life of Riley-o
   Such a lot of populo.
              [*Ritornelle is repeated.*]

   Per totam terram videmus
   Grandam vogam ubi sumus;
   Vere dico, bene cautus
   Omnes sunt so mad about us.
Totus mundus, currens ad nostros
         remedios,
   Nos regardat sicut Deos;
   Et nostris prescriptionibus
Principes et reges submissos videtis.
              [*A second ritornelle.*]

Well then, est nostrae sapientiae,
Boni sensus atque prudentiae
   Earnestemente laborare
   A nos bene conservare
In tali credito, voga, et honore,
Et takum care a non recevere
   In nostro docto corpore
   Quam personas capabiles,
   Et totas dignas providere
   Has plazas honorabiles.
              [*Second ritornelle is repeated.*]

That's why nunc convocati estis;
   Et credo quod findabitis
   Dignam materiam medici
   In savanti homine here you see,
   And him, in thingis omnibus

Dono ad interrogandum,
Et thoroughly examinandum
Vostris capacitatibus.
[*He sits down. A third and longer ritornelle.*]

FIRST DOCTOR   Si mihi dat licentiam Dominus Praeses,
Et tanti docti Doctores,
Et also-presentes illustres,
Most savanti Bacheliero
Quem estimo et honoro,
Demandabo causam et rationem quare
Opium facit dormire.

[*He sits down.* BÉRALDE *signals to* ARGAN, *the* BACHE-
LIERUS. *He rises.* BÉRALDE *prompts him.*]

ARGAN   Mihi a docto Doctore
Demandatur causam et rationem quare
Opium facit dormire.
And to that respondeo
Quia est in eo
Virtus dormitiva
Cujus est natura
Sensus tranquillizare.

CHORUS   Bene, bene, bene, bene respondere!
Dignus, dignus est entrare
In nostro docto corpore.

SECOND DOCTOR   Cum permissione Domini Praesidis,
Doctissimae Facultatis,
Et totius his nostris actis
Companiae presentis,
Demandabo tibi, docte Bacheliere,
Quae sunt remedia
Quae in maladia
Called hydropisia
Convenit facere.

ARGAN   Give 'emam enemam,
'N'enemam bleedemam,

'N'enemam purgemam.

CHORUS   Bene, bene, bene, bene respondere!
                  Dignus, dignus est entrare
                  In nostro docto corpore.

THIRD DOCTOR   Si paret OK by Domine Praesidi,
                  Doctissimae Facultati,
                  Et companiae presenti,
                  Demandabo tibi, docte Bacheliere,
                  Quae remedia eticis
                  Pulmonicis, atque asmaticis
                  You finda fittinga facere.

ARGAN   Give 'emam enemam,
                  'N'enemam bleedemam,
                  'N'enemam purgemam.

CHORUS   Bene, bene, bene, bene respondere!
                  Dignus, dignus est entrare
                  In nostro docto corpore.

FOURTH DOCTOR   Super illas maladias
                  Doctus Bachelierus dixit marvelias;
                  But si non annoyo Dominum Praesi-
                        dem,
                  Doctissimam Facultatem
                  Et totam honorabilem
                  Companiam listeninginam,
                  Faciam illi unam quaestionem.
                  Yesterdayo maladus unus
                  Landedavit in meas manus;
                  Habet grandam fievram cum redoubla-
                        mentis,
                  Grandem dolorem capitis,
                  Et grandem malum in the sidis,
                  Cum granda difficultate
                  Et troubla de respirare.
                  Be so goodo mihi dire,
                  Docte Bacheliere,
                  Quid illi facere?

ARGAN   Give 'emam enemam,

	'N'enemam bleedemam,
	'N'enemam purgemam.
FIFTH DOCTOR	But if maladia
	Obstinativa
	Non vult get wella
	Quid illi facere?
ARGAN	Give 'emam enemam,
	'N'enemam bleedemam,
	'N'enemam purgemam;
	'N'enemam bleedemam purgemam againemam.
CHORUS	Bene, bene, bene, bene respondere!
	Dignus, dignus est entrare
	In nostro docto corpore.

PRESIDING OFFICER [*rises solemnly; other doctors rise also*]

         Juras guardare statuta
         Per Facultatem praescripta
         Cum sensu et jugeamento?

ARGAN [*extending right hand*] Juro.

PRESIDING OFFICER	Essere in omnibus
	Consultationibus
	Ancieni opinione,
	Aut bono
	Aut baddo?
ARGAN	Juro.
PRESIDING OFFICER	Et never make uso
	Of remediis anyis
	Exceptus those doctae Facultatis,
	Though maladus should croakere
	Et mori de suo malo?
ARGAN	Juro.
PRESIDING OFFICER	Ego, cum isto boneto
	Venerabili et docto,
	Dono tibi et concedo
	Virtutem et puissanciam
	Medicandi,

Purgandi,
Bleedandi,
Pierçandi,
Cuttandi,
Slashandi,
Et murderandi
Impune per totam terram.

[PRESIDING OFFICER *and companions seat themselves.*
First apothecary invests ARGAN *with his gown, to music.*
The second puts on his wig, the third his toque. Ballet.
All the surgeons and apothecaries salute ARGAN. *He*
opens roll of paper and reads.]

ARGAN

Grandes doctores doctrinae
Of rhubarb et senna,
In me it would be ridiculosissimum,
Absurdum, ineptum,
If I undertookum
To give vobis gloriam.
I'd superimposo
Lux to the sunno,
Stellas to caelo,
Undas Oceano,
Rosas to summero.
Kindly recipito
My gratitudo,
Molto obbligato corpori docto.
Vobis, vobis debeo
More than to nature and patri meo.
Natura et pater meus
Hominem me habent factum;
But vos me, what's a lot more,
Habetis factum medicum;
Honor, favor, et gratia
Qui in hoc corde right here
Imprintant gratitudinem
Qui endurerit in saecula.

[He bows. The doctors rise; all join in chorus.]

CHORUS

> Vivat, vivat, vivat, vivat, a hundred
>   times vivat
> Novus Doctor, qui tam bene parlat!
> Mille, mille annis et eatet et drinket
> Et bleedet et killet!

[Music. The doctors salute ARGAN and exit. The surgeons and apothecaries dance and sing, to the accompaniment of handclapping and the clinking of apothecaries' mortars.]

SURGEON

> May he see doctas
> Suas prescriptiones
> Omnium chirurgorum
> Et apothicarum
> Fill up the shoppos!

CHORUS

> Vivat, vivat, vivat, vivat, a hundred
>   times vivat
> Novus Doctor, qui tam bene parlat!
> Mille, mille annis et eatet et drinket
> Et bleedet et killet!

SURGEON

> May toti anni
> Be to him boni
> Et favorabiles;
> Et may he have plenty
> Of pestas and poxas,
> Fievras, pleuresias,
> Hemorrhagias, et dysenterias!

CHORUS

> Vivat, vivat, vivat, vivat, a hundred
>   times vivat
> Novus Doctor, qui tam bene parlat!
> Mille, mille annis et eatet et drinket
> Et bleedet et killet!

[Dancers exit according to their rank. The members of the family salute ARGAN, who salutes the public.]

CURTAIN

BIBLIOGRAPHY

The standard definitive French edition of Molière's complete works is that by Despois and Mesnard, in the series of *Les Grands Écrivains de la France*, 13 vols. (Paris, 1873-1927).

By far the best acting edition of *Le Malade imaginaire* is that by Pierre Valde, Éditions du Seuil (Paris, 1946). This gives invaluable help on staging and production.

There are innumerable biographies and criticisms in French. Probably the best compendious work is Gustave Michaut's three volumes (Paris, Hachette, 1922-25). A charming brief appreciation is Maurice Donnay's *Molière* (Paris, Fayart, 1911). For the state of medical knowledge and practice in Molière's time, see M. Raynaud, *Les Médecins au temps de Molière* (Paris, Didier, 1863). An excellent recent medical study of Molière's own case is that by René Thuillier, *La Vie maladive de Molière* (Paris, 1932).

In English, the best all-round book on Molière is John Palmer's *Molière* (New York, Brewer and Warren, 1930).